# Disordered Eating

## Series Editor: Cara Acred

## Volume 321

**Independence Educational Publishers**

First published by Independence Educational Publishers

The Studio, High Green

Great Shelford

Cambridge CB22 5EG

England

© Independence 2017

ISBN-13: 978 1 86168 771 5

## Printed in Great Britain

Zenith Print Group

# Contents

# Introduction

*DISORDERED EATING* is Volume 321 in the **ISSUES** series. The aim of the series is to offer current, diverse information about important issues in our world, from a UK perspective.

### ABOUT TITLE

The term 'eating disorders' now encompasses much more than just anorexia and bulimia. Eating Disorders Not Otherwise Specified, orthorexia and even protorexia are become more and more talked about. This book explores all of these forms of problem eating, as well as potential treatments. It also looks at topical issues such as the dangers behind the clean eating craze and whether, in fact, this encourages the development of eating disorders among vulnerable people.

### OUR SOURCES

Titles in the **ISSUES** series are designed to function as educational resource books, providing a balanced overview of a specific subject.

The information in our books is comprised of facts, articles and opinions from many different sources, including:

⇨ Newspaper reports and opinion pieces

⇨ Website factsheets

⇨ Magazine and journal articles

⇨ Statistics and surveys

⇨ Government reports

⇨ Literature from special interest groups.

### A NOTE ON CRITICAL EVALUATION

Because the information reprinted here is from a number of different sources, readers should bear in mind the origin of the text and whether the source is likely to have a particular bias when presenting information (or when conducting their research). It is hoped that, as you read about the many aspects of the issues explored in this book, you will critically evaluate the information presented.

It is important that you decide whether you are being presented with facts or opinions. Does the writer give a biased or unbiased report? If an opinion is being expressed, do you agree with the writer? Is there potential bias to the 'facts' or statistics behind an article?

### ASSIGNMENTS

In the back of this book, you will find a selection of assignments designed to help you engage with the articles you have been reading and to explore your own opinions. Some tasks will take longer than others and

## Useful weblinks

www.berealcampaign.co.uk

www.beateatingdisorders.co.uk

www.bodywhys.ie

www.theconversation.com

www.eating-disorders.org.uk

www.eatingdisorders.org.au

www.theguardian.com

www.huffingtonpost.co.uk

www.ibtimes.co.uk

www.mind.org.uk

www.mnn.com

mosaicscience.com

www.newbridge-health.org.uk

www.nhs.uk

there is a mixture of design, writing and research-based activities that you can complete alone or in a group.

### FURTHER RESEARCH

At the end of each article we have listed its source and a website that you can visit if you would like to conduct your own research. Please remember to critically evaluate any sources that you consult and consider whether the information you are viewing is accurate and unbiased.

# Eating disorders

Eating disorders are characterised by an abnormal attitude towards food that causes someone to change their eating habits and behaviour.

A person with an eating disorder may focus excessively on their weight and shape, leading them to make unhealthy choices about food with damaging results to their health.

## *Types of eating disorders*

Eating disorders include a range of conditions that can affect someone physically, psychologically and socially. The most common eating disorders are:

⇨ anorexia nervosa – when a person tries to keep their weight as low as possible; for example, by starving themselves or exercising excessively

⇨ bulimia – when a person goes through periods of binge eating and is then deliberately sick or uses laxatives (medication to help empty the bowels) to try to control their weight

⇨ binge eating disorder (BED) – when a person feels compelled to overeat large amounts of food in a short space of time.

Some people, particularly those who are young, may be diagnosed with an eating disorder not otherwise specified (EDNOS). This means you have some, but not all, of the typical signs of eating disorders like anorexia or bulimia.

## *What causes eating disorders?*

Eating disorders are often blamed on the social pressure to be thin, as young people in particular feel they should look a certain way. However, the causes are usually more complex.

An eating disorder may be associated with biological, genetic or environmental factors combined with a particular event that triggers the disorder. There may also be other factors that maintain the illness.

Risk factors that can increase the likelihood of a person having an eating disorder include:

⇨ having a family history of eating disorders, depression or substance misuse

⇨ being criticised for their eating habits, body shape or weight

⇨ being overly concerned with being slim, particularly if combined with pressure to be slim from society or for a job – for example, ballet dancers, models or athletes

⇨ certain underlying characteristics – for example, having an obsessive personality, an anxiety disorder, low self-esteem or being a perfectionist

⇨ particular experiences, such as sexual or emotional abuse or the death of someone special

⇨ difficult relationships with family members or friends

⇨ stressful situations – for example, problems at work, school or university.

## *Do I have an eating disorder?*

Doctors sometimes use a questionnaire to help identify people who may have an eating disorder. The questionnaire asks the following five questions:

⇨ Do you make yourself sick because you feel uncomfortably full?

⇨ Do you worry you have lost control over how much you eat?

⇨ Have you recently lost more than one stone (six kilograms) in a three-month period?

⇨ Do you believe yourself to be fat when others say you are too thin?

⇨ Would you say food dominates your life?

⇨ If you answer "yes" to two or more of these questions, you may have an eating disorder.

## *Spotting an eating disorder in others*

It can often be very difficult to identify that a loved one or friend has developed an eating disorder.

Warning signs to look out for include:

- missing meals
- complaining of being fat, even though they have a normal weight or are underweight
- repeatedly weighing themselves and looking at themselves in the mirror
- making repeated claims that they've already eaten, or they'll shortly be going out to eat somewhere else and avoiding eating at home
- cooking big or complicated meals for other people, but eating little or none of the food themselves
- only eating certain low-calorie foods in your presence, such as lettuce or celery
- feeling uncomfortable or refusing to eat in public places, such as at a restaurant
- the use of 'pro-anorexia' websites

It can be difficult to know what to do if you're concerned about a friend or family member. It's not unusual for someone with an eating disorder to be secretive and defensive about their eating and their weight, and they may deny being unwell.

## Who's affected by eating disorders?

A 2015 report commissioned by Beat estimates more than 725,000 people in the UK are affected by an eating disorder. Eating disorders tend to be more common in certain age groups, but they can affect people of any age.

Around one in 250 women and one in 2,000 men will experience anorexia nervosa at some point. The condition usually develops around the age of 16 or 17.

Bulimia is around two to three times more common than anorexia nervosa, and 90% of people with the condition are female. It usually develops around the age of 18 or 19.

Binge eating affects males and females equally and usually appears later in life, between the ages of 30 and 40. As it's difficult to precisely define binge eating, it's not clear how widespread it is, but it's estimated to affect around 5% of the adult population.

## Treating eating disorders

If an eating disorder isn't treated, it can have a negative impact on someone's job or schoolwork, and can disrupt relationships with family members and friends. The physical effects of an eating disorder can sometimes be fatal.

Treatment for eating disorders is available, although recovery can take a long time. It's important that the person affected wants to get better, and the support of family and friends is invaluable.

Treatment usually involves monitoring a person's physical health while helping them deal with the underlying psychological causes. This may involve:

- using self-help manuals and books, possibly under guidance from a therapist or another healthcare professional
- cognitive behavioural therapy (CBT) – therapy that focuses on changing how a person thinks about a situation, which in turn will affect how they act
- interpersonal psychotherapy – a talking therapy that focuses on relationship-based issues
- dietary counselling – a talking therapy to help a person maintain a healthy diet
- psychodynamic therapy or cognitive analytic therapy (CAT) – therapy that focuses on how a person's personality and life experiences influence their current thoughts, feelings, relationships and behaviour
- family therapy – therapy involving the family discussing how the eating disorder has affected them and their relationships
- medication – for example, a type of antidepressant called selective serotonin reuptake inhibitors (SSRIs) may be used to treat bulimia nervosa or binge eating

There's a range of other healthcare services that can help, such as support and self-help groups, and personal and telephone counselling services.

*Page last reviewed: 29/06/2015*

*Next review due: 01/06/2018*

- The above information is reprinted with kind permission from NHS Choices. Please visit www.nhs.uk for further information.

*© NHS Choices 2017*

## Eating Disorder Not Otherwise Specified (EDNOS)

"A person with Eating Disorder Not Otherwise Specified (EDNOS) may present with many of the symptoms of other eating disorders such as Anorexia Nervosa or Bulimia Nervosa but will not meet the full criteria for diagnosis of these disorders. This does not mean that the person has a less serious eating disorder. EDNOS is a serious mental illness that occurs in adults, adolescents and children. 40% – 60% of people who seek treatment for an eating disorder have EDNOS."

*Source: National Eating Disorders Collaboration*
*www.nedc.com.au*

# Eating problems

### What is an eating problem?

An eating problem is any relationship with food that you find difficult.

Food plays an important part in our lives and most of us will spend time thinking about what we eat. Sometimes we may try to eat more healthily, have cravings, eat more than usual or lose our appetite. Changing your eating habits every now and again is normal.

But if food and eating feels like it's taking over your life then it may become a problem.

Lots of people think that if you have an eating problem you will be over- or underweight, and that being a certain weight is always associated with a specific eating problem. This is a myth. Anyone, regardless of age, gender or weight, can be affected by eating problems.

**"Food was like poison to me. It resembled all the negativity in my life. It made me feel weighed down by impurity, dirtiness, ugliness and selfishness. My body shape made me miserable and I spent all day everyday thinking about how great life would be if I was skinny"**

If you have an eating problem you might:

⇨ restrict the amount of food you eat

⇨ eat more than you need or feel out of control when you eat

⇨ eat a lot in secret

⇨ feel very anxious about eating or digesting food

⇨ eat lots of food in response to difficult emotions (when you don't feel physically hungry)

⇨ only eat certain types of food or stick to a rigid set of diet rules and feel very anxious and upset if you have to eat something different

⇨ do things to get rid of what you eat (purging)

⇨ stick to rigid rules around what you can and can't eat and how food should look – and feel very upset if you break those rules

⇨ feel strongly repulsed at the idea of eating certain foods

⇨ eat things that are not really food

⇨ be scared of certain types of food or eating in public

⇨ think about food and eating a lot or all the time

⇨ compare your body to other people's and think about their shape or size a lot

⇨ check, test and weigh your body a lot – and base your self-worth on how much you weigh or whether you pass your checks and tests.

### What's the difference between an eating problem and an eating disorder?

An eating disorder is a medical diagnosis based on your eating patterns, and medical tests on your weight, blood and body mass index (BMI).

An eating problem is any relationship with food that you find difficult. This can be just as hard to live with as a diagnosed eating disorder.

### How might eating problems affect my life?

Eating problems are not just about food. They can be about difficult things and painful feelings, which you may be finding hard to express, face or resolve. Focusing on food can be a way of disguising these problems, even from yourself.

Eating problems can affect you in lots of ways. You might:

⇨ find it difficult to concentrate and feel tired a lot

- find that controlling food or eating has become the most important thing in your life
- feel depressed and anxious
- feel ashamed or guilty and scared of other people finding out
- feel distant from friends or family who do not know how you feel or who are frustrated and upset that they can't do more to help you
- avoid social occasions, dates and restaurants or eating in public
- find it hard to be spontaneous, to travel or to go anywhere new
- find that your appearance has changed
- find that other people comment on your appearance in ways you find difficult
- find that you are bullied or teased about food and eating
- develop short- or long-term physical health problems
- find that you have to drop out of school or college, leave work or stop doing things you enjoy.

**"I never looked 'ill'. When I read about eating disorders it was always girls with acute anorexia. Because that wasn't me, I felt like my behaviour was just a bizarre quirk I'd made up. Ironically, it felt like I couldn't even do self-destruction properly... I felt like a fraud and came down on myself harder"**

You might find that other people focus a lot on the effect eating problems can have on your body, or that they only think you have a problem if your body looks different to how they think it should be, and that they don't really understand how complicated things are for you.

It's also possible to have problems with eating and keep them hidden –

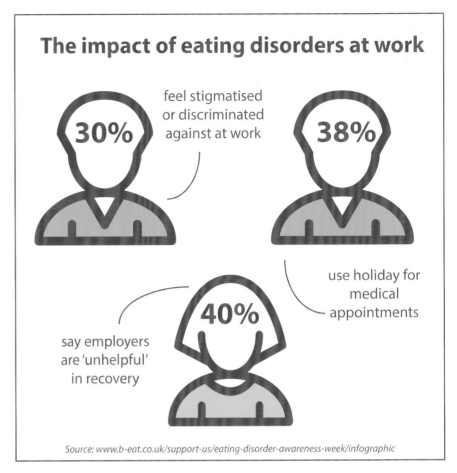

## The impact of eating disorders at work

**30%** feel stigmatised or discriminated against at work

**38%** use holiday for medical appointments

**40%** say employers are 'unhelpful' in recovery

*Source: www.b-eat.co.uk/support-us/eating-disorder-awareness-week/infographic*

sometimes for a very long time. You might not even be sure that your issues with food and eating are a 'problem', as it may feel like just part of your everyday life. Some people don't seek help because they think their problem is not serious enough or they are not 'good enough' at their eating problem.

But if your relationship with food and eating is affecting your life, it is OK to seek help. It doesn't matter how much you weigh or what your body looks like.

## Eating problems and other mental health problems

Lots of people with eating problems also have other mental health problems, such as depression, anxiety or obsessive-compulsive disorders. Food is one of many mediums through which anxiety, depression or obsessive-compulsive behaviours can be expressed. Body dysmorphic disorder is an anxiety disorder linked to body image, which can also lead to eating problems.

For some people, eating problems are linked to self-harm – you may see your eating problem as a form of self-harm, and you may hurt yourself in other ways too. For others they're related to body image and self-esteem. And for others eating problems can be more like a phobia of certain foods.

My eating disorder has always gone hand in hand with depression and anxiety in such a way that they haven't felt like distinct, discrete illnesses but like one issue.

### Suicidal feelings

You may have thoughts about death or suicidal feelings. You might feel that you want to die, or that it is the only way to escape your eating problem. This can be very frightening and make you feel alone.

For support with these feelings you can contact the Samaritans who are available 24 hours a day. If you are under 35, you might find it helpful to talk to Papyrus.

*© Mind 2017. This information is taken from the Mind resource* Understanding Eating Problems. *The full version is available from mind.org.uk*

# Eating disorder statistics

## How many people in the UK have an eating disorder?

*The Costs of Eating Disorders – Social, Health and Economic Impacts* report, commissioned by Beat and produced by PwC in February 2015, estimates that 1.25 million people in the UK are affected by an eating disorder – using a more robust methodology than previous studies.

The National Institute of Health and Clinical Excellence estimates around 11% of those affected by an eating disorder are male.

Recent research from the NHS information centre showed that up to 6.4% of adults displayed signs of an eating disorder (Adult Psychiatric Morbidity Survey, 2007). This research suggested that up to 25% of those showing signs of an eating disorder were male.

The Health and Care Information Centre published figures in February 2014 that showed an 8% rise in the number of inpatient hospital admissions in the 12 months previous to October 2013. *The Costs of Eating Disorders* report found that this is indicative of the trend in increasing prevalence over time: a 34% increase in admissions since 2005–06 – approximately 7% each year.

### SCOFF questionnaire:

Do you ever make yourself **Sick** because you feel uncomfortably full?

Do you worry you have lost **Control** over how much you eat?

Have you recently lost more than **One** stone in a three-month period?

Do you believe yourself to be **Fat** when others say you are too thin?

Would you say that **Food** dominates your life?

## Which eating disorder is the most common?

The latest version of the DSM (Diagnostic and Statistical Manual of Mental Disorders) cites the main eating disorders as anorexia, bulimia and binge eating disorder (BED), eliminating EDNOS (eating disorder not otherwise specified).

Before the latest change in diagnostic criteria, it was estimated that of those with eating disorders, 10% were anorexic, 40% were bulimic and the rest fall into the EDNOS category which included BED.

## At what age do people develop eating disorders?

Although many eating disorders develop during adolescence, it is not at all unusual for people to develop eating disorders earlier or later in life. In fact, we are aware of cases of anorexia in children as young as six and some research reports cases developing in women in their 70s. Outside of the stereotypical age bracket, people are less likely to be appropriately diagnosed due to a lack of understanding and awareness of eating disorders in these age groups.

## How long do eating disorders last?

Research carried out in Australia suggests that the average duration of anorexia is eight years and five years for bulimia. However, these illnesses can also become severe and enduring, lasting for many years and having a hugely debilitating effect on the sufferers and their families. The sooner someone gets the treatment they need, the more likely they are to make a full recovery.

## Is it possible to recover from an eating disorder?

Yes. We are lucky enough to work with some very inspirational people and we hear some very uplifting stories of recovery. Research suggests that around 46% of anorexia patients fully recover, 33% improving and 20% remaining chronically ill. Similar research into bulimia suggests that 45% make a full recovery, 27% improve considerably and 23% suffer chronically.

## How devastating are eating disorders?

Anorexia has the highest mortality rate of any psychiatric disorder, from medical complications associated with the illness as well as suicide. Research has found that 20% of anorexia sufferers will die prematurely from their illness. Bulimia is also associated with severe medical complications, and binge eating disorder sufferers often experience the medical complications associated with obesity. In every case, eating disorders severely affect the quality of life of the sufferer and those that care for them.

## How should people with eating disorders seek help?

The first port of call for a sufferer should always be their making an appointment with their GP. The Beat Helpline is available for support and information, and can give people suggestions for how to approach their doctor. After seeking advice from your GP, it can be useful to search Beat's HelpFinder to find specialised eating disorder help near you.

## Do eating disorders run in families?

Eating disorders are complex with no one sole cause, but we know from research that individuals might be predisposed due to their genetic or biological make up.

Some research has found that female relatives of anorexia sufferers were

11.4 times more likely to suffer from anorexia compared to relatives of unaffected participants. For female relatives of those with bulimia, the likelihood of developing bulimia was 3.7 times that of those with unaffected relatives.

It is not yet clear how much of this link between family members is genetic and how much is due to environmental factors.

## How can you tell if someone has an eating disorder?

You cannot tell if someone has an eating disorder just by looking at them. While it is true that some sufferers of anorexia are severely emaciated, some are not, and the majority of eating disorder sufferers do not have anorexia. Those suffering from bulimia may be within the normal weight range or may be overweight, while those with binge eating disorder are often overweight.

Professor John Morgan at Leeds Partnership NHS Foundation Trust designed the SCOFF screening tool to indicate a possible eating disorder. A score of two or more positive answers is a positive screen.

⇨ The above information is reprinted with kind permission from Beat. Please visit www.beateatingdisorders.org.uk for further information.

*© Beat 2017*

# Avoidant/Restrictive Food Intake Disorder

Avoidant/Restrictive Food Intake Disorder (ARFID) is a diagnosis that has been acknowledged relatively recently (in 2013). It may be informally known as Selective Eating Disorder (SED). ARFID may occur during childhood, but it can also develop in adults. Currently, little is known about effective treatments and interventions and the course of illness for individuals who develop ARFID. Other unknown factors include the age at which ARFID develops and whether or not it presents as a risk factor for later-onset eating disorders.

In ARFID, a person may experience food disturbances to the point that they do not meet their appropriate nutritional and/or energy needs. This may be underlined by factors such as avoidance due to the sensory characteristics of food, a lack of interest in eating or food, or worries about the consequences of eating.

Individuals affected by ARFID may present with:

⇨ Clinically significant restrictive eating leading to weight loss, or a lack of weight gain

⇨ Nutritional deficiencies

⇨ Reliance on tube feeding and oral nutritional supplements

⇨ Disturbances in psychosocial functioning.

Research has also identified behaviours and difficulties such as:

⇨ Food avoidance

⇨ Restrictive eating

⇨ Selective eating since childhood

⇨ Decreased appetite

⇨ Abdominal pain

⇨ A heightened fear of vomiting and/or choking

⇨ Possible food texture issues

⇨ Generalised anxiety

⇨ Gastrointestinal symptoms.

There may be some body image concerns, though different to those seen in cases of anorexia and bulimia. Those with ARFID may be less likely to report typical eating disorder behaviours such as purging and excessive exercise.

Research has identified some possible contributory factors. In children, there may be a fear of physical illness related to shape/weight for example, high cholesterol and/or obesity leading to heart disease. Other children who were underweight due to feeding and eating disturbances have reported teasing from peers.

⇨ The above information is reprinted with kind permission from Bodywhys. Please visit www.bodywhys.ie for further information.

*© Bodywhys 2017*

# Phases of restrictive eating disorders

## Information for parents/loved ones.

### Stage one of an ED. I'm not so bad, I'm certainly not ill – leave me alone

This is where someone has lost some weight and it doesn't seem to be stopping. You have probably told them how much better they look but now it's time to stop. The loved one isn't 'too thin' but you are alarmed about their eating habits. They are eating on their own much more, and they have probably become vegetarian which is an excuse to eat less fat and to feel more pure. This desire for "purity" is one of the early signs of anorexia. Yes, many people go on diets, and Yes, many people become vegetarian for all sorts of reasons. But most dieters cannot wait to stop their diet and they do not become afraid to eat. Normal dieters do not get enraged when someone tries to persuade them to eat some food.

In stage one when someone isn't absolutely underweight quite yet, they are hearing a voice in their head which convinces them that they will feel much better if they lose just a little more weight. The problem is that this voice doesn't go away. No matter how much weight they lose, it's always just a little more.

In stage one of an eating disorder your loved one knows there is something wrong but shuts this knowing away. They convince you and themselves that they are fine, they feel much better, they can run 100 miles. Of course they do not have anorexia because anorexics are thinner and anorexics aren't hungry – are they? Some people call this "denial" but they are actually terrified to change.

Stage one is anorexia on the cusp of being something bad. Because it isn't too bad yet, everyone hopes that it will just go away. Nine times out of ten, its going to get much worse. It's going to last a while and it may – for an indefinite while – become a serious mental affliction.

### Solution for stage one

Can anyone do anything to stop the decline? Sadly I believe the answer is "no". The eating disorder has captured the person because they already have deficiencies in their capacity to cope with life. These 'deficiencies' have not been previously obvious and their ability to lose weight feels like the first thing they can be proud of. The patient will be unwilling and unable to give restriction up and learn how to 'be stronger'. Carers must know that threats and warnings increase resistance and denial. *It won't happen to me and I don't care*.

If I see a patient in stage one of their problem I can do my best to persuade them that treatment will make them happier and stronger – not just put on weight. I may help to change the way the Voice speaks to them. I can listen to their underlying pain which needs to be expressed. This will absolutely have a good effect and it may stop the illness from getting worse, but there is no quick fix and I have to work with carers so that they are fully prepared for what they may have to do. We will need to get schools and colleges into the treatment loop no matter how much the loved one says "no".

### Stage two of an ED. I think I have a problem but I can manage it on my own, it's not so bad so go away

Stages one and two are not distinct, one melts into the other quite fast. This is where you become really worried about your loved one and the more worried you are the more your loved one pushes you away. You stand outside the locked bedroom door; please come out, join us and eat something. Can't you see how awful you are looking! Do you have to go running at 6am every day? Talk to us, talk to us. Come and see the GP. No, get lost! F- Off!

In stage two weight is being lost slowly or quickly and no one can deny it is just a phase. He/she will eat no fat and no carbs; everything is on their forbidden list. The loved one is only listening to the Voice inside their head, *lose more weight, you're doing well*, but *you're still fat, you're ugly and no one understands*. By now they are sinking into their own world where no one else belongs, they probably aren't seeing their friends and they're spending time alone. They are attached to their eating disorder as if it were a marriage, while insisting nothing's wrong, they are just a little tired and stressed.

You as a carer cannot underestimate how many benefits they are getting from having their eating disorder. Yes, they feel tired and cold and painfully hungry and miserable. But he/she is getting a lot of pluses from their eating disorder even though they aren't aware of it yet. This has become a way of helping them to feel special, to feel different from others, to feel superior in the only way they know how. The eating disorder is useful in helping them to avoid things in life they cannot cope with, like managing painful feelings or doing their exams. The eating disorder is useful because it can bring warring parents together and it is useful because it says to others "I'm in pain" (although I'm not sure why).

So don't expect your loved one to be a willing participant in therapy. They will explain that they are terrified of putting on weight. They believe with absolute conviction that any departure from their diet systems will make them gain weight and it will never stop. They are terrified of having to get on with life with all the horrible feelings that existed before they started losing weight. You say *it's easy just eat something please*. The Voice in their head says, if you do eat, you are weak and greedy. They are in a hopeless trap and restriction can increase.

If I see someone in stage two, the ED is very well entrenched. To know how serious it is, I have to look at other things like how fast weight is being lost, how little are they eating, are they young or older, and what their childhood experiences have been. Are there other mental issues present like depression and anxiety in early life. We are able to predict how serious this illness could become and we must arm carers with some of the weapons they need to cope with and manage the entity which has captured the consciousness of their loved one. Workshops and guidance for carers will be crucial, and they must know what to expect. Safety strategies must be put in place in case there is a risk to life.

Is there anything a therapist can do at this stage? Yes and no. Starvation stops your loved one from hearing because the brain doesn't work as it should. The priority is to set in motion what will happen if someone does collapse. We therapists can do motivational work, to help the captive describe all the ways in which the Eating Problem is their friend. We can help the captive see how the ED will get in the way of what other things are important in their life. We can help the captive understand that they are more than what they weigh, but this kind of understanding will take time to sink in.

### Stage three of an ED. I know I'm ill but I don't care, I can't eat and you can't make me. I can't make myself either

This is what is going on inside the head of your loved one like a vicious running tape recorder.

*My eating disorder is like an addiction, I can't stop, when I eat I am not myself.*

*I have this voice in my head that talks to me. It tells me what to do. It tells me I am fat and worthless and that I am not allowed to eat because I don't deserve food.*

*...inside I am broken and fragile. I'm slowly crumbling. I'm slowly fading away and becoming invisible and soon I will be forgotten. I'm dead inside and gone but outside there is still a body you see. I really hope I will die because the world will be a better place without me and there will be no pain. I've tried to smile but behind my smile is a world of pain.*

*I don't like looking in mirrors because if I look inside them I feel that my ugliness is going to break the mirror. I cry every time I look in the mirror.*

*My eating disorder has become my world and I really don't care about anything else. I spend every minute thinking about calories and ignoring the hunger and the dizziness and the heartbeats that quicken to a scary rate. I can't change even if I tried and even if I wanted to. I will always have this and it's my identity.*

Your loved one is very low weight and it goes up and down, they are depressed and obsessive, angry and sometimes violent toward loved ones.

They say they are going to get better but it just doesn't happen. They know they have a serious mental condition but they have eroded into a sense of helplessness. They just have to see someone thinner or iller than themselves to be convinced that they are not so bad and they are provoked into a need to compete to be the illest and the thinnest in the room. The illness makes them lie, hide food and deceive. They try to fake their weights. You have lost the person you once knew and you are grieving the life that could and should have been. At times you think you're going mad. You are suffering, and they don't really care – although they say they do.

The Voice is now the only thing that they can hear. The Voice is telling them that if they try to get away it will punish them. The Voice is stronger than you and stronger than anyone else. No matter how much the illness hurts them, they are getting so much from it. They really do feel superior to people who have to eat – like you and like their therapist. They do not wish to be fat like you – and their therapist. Their feelings are blunted. They are getting attention, although at the same time they don't want it; yet they do the very things that guarantee they are going to get it.

Thinking in all stages of anorexia but particularly this stage is dominated by rules. The rules are seen as the solution to the person's problems whereas we see the rules as the problem because they are severe, irrational and inflexible. However, it is only by following the rules completely that the person experiences control and relief.

*I live my life by them. I must weigh under a certain number. I must eat less than a certain number of calories. I must be smaller than a certain dress size. I must eat my food in a certain order. I must leave a certain amount of time between meals. I must not eat after a certain time... (just listing these is exhausting!)... I must lose at least this amount. I must run for a certain amount of minutes (at least).*

*That's the thing with the rules. They always demand at least, you're never allowed to do less than the rules specify, only more. I know that these rules shrink the limits in which you allow yourself to exist, as they steal more and more of your freedom. And the more I starve myself the more the rules grow.*

If I see someone in this phase of the illness, I will not be trusted. Anorexia puts up a barrier so that I will not be able to find the person under the protection of their captor. I have to find a way inside to help them find and understand the pain that brought the illness in, in the first place. I will speak directly to the Voice which I will separate from the person it speaks to. I will reassure them that recovery is holistic, it is physical, emotional and spiritual. I will insist that eating more or less is not altogether my concern but... no ifs and no buts without eating more we will wait forever for things to change. In this way the anorexia has nothing against me to fight. Safety strategies must always be in place in case of risk to life and some may die but most do not.

## Stage four of the ED: a turning point

In this stage the restricting person has – for any number of reasons – decided that they do not wish to live like this any more. You may not know that they have changed because their behaviour has not changed. It may take a very long time before it does. It can take seven years or even more to reach the turning point.

They want to change but are deeply afraid of change. They want to change to feel better, to be able to move around without fatigue, to get on with life and to stop the suffering of their families. They realise dimly that they are more than what they weigh. It is as if they have seen the light but the light may still be dim. It may be a mistake to assume that they are ready and willing to eat... The Voice is still there and opposing the voice is the hardest thing for them to do. In some respects it is far easier to stay ill. We have to show that we can help them to fight the Voice and not just be eating bullies.

If I see someone in this phase of the illness, the person is taking some action to try and be well, but they are still deeply ambivalent. The sufferer needs the informed help of a sensitive

dietician, together with a lot of useful information for them to digest. They need help with their emotions to be able to tolerate bad and dangerous feelings which ordinary life must bring. Only with some nourishment will they be able to do the therapy which will help them feel that life is worth living and that they are not the bad awful people they irrationally believe they are. They need to learn to feel connection with loved ones, with other people and also in a spiritual sense. They may need to make amends to feel whole and worthy again. This phase of the illness is very delicate and many people relapse before they are finally able to say goodbye to their illness. For some people the job is just too hard and they make a bargain with their anorexia. They may say I am better now but I will only eat food which is really healthy for me, or I will take up running marathons.

## Stage five of the ED – living afterwards, maintaining change

Well but scarred. Does anorexia ever really go? Your loved one might be well but still has the sensitivity and the emotional vulnerability that led to the illness in the first place. We have to hope that good caring therapy is dealing with this so that the person no longer needs to restrict food to be able to cope with life. They may miss their 'friend' and wish at times that it was there to hide behind when life gets tough. There will be times when some of the old behaviour creeps back, under the radar. *I think I must start going to the gym. I think I'm allergic to wheat and need to go without it for a while.*

Part of therapy is to help the loved one be alert for times when the Voice comes back. Then we must reach down to the stress and the feelings which are not being managed well. We must help the person see that the only friends welcome in their life are those who are good for them and care for them properly. The Voice is the abusive friend, who should be shunned.

Carers need to know that most people do recover from a restrictive ED and move on. They have to learn to stop living on eggshells, but at the same time must be careful about what they say. Words like "You look so much better", or "You looked awful back then", are interpreted as "You look fat, You were doing well before". The therapist must coach the patient to be able to hear such statements without making these emotional interpretations. Therapists need to learn to let go and teach the person to do it on their own.

If any of our articles moves you or you want to know more, or get some help, just get in touch on 0845 838 2040 or admin@ncfed.com.

⇨ The above information is reprinted with kind permission from the National Centre for Eating Disorders. Please visit www.eating-disorders.org.uk for further information.

# Disordered eating and dieting

**D**isordered eating refers to a wide range of abnormal eating behaviours, many of which are shared with diagnosed eating disorders. The main thing differentiating disordered eating from an eating disorder is the level of severity and frequency of behaviours.

## "Dieting can lead to feelings of guilt over 'lack of self control', low self esteem, a poor body image and obsessive thoughts and behaviours surrounding food"

Disordered eating can have a negative impact on a person's emotional, social and physical wellbeing. It may lead to fatigue, malnutrition or poor concentration. It can affect someone's social life (when socialising is restricted due to anxiety around food/eating), and can lead to anxiety and depression.

Disordered eating behaviours and attitudes include:

⇨ Binge eating

⇨ Dieting

⇨ Skipping meals regularly

⇨ Self-induced vomiting

⇨ Obsessive calorie counting

⇨ Self-worth based on body shape and weight

⇨ Misusing laxatives or diurectics

⇨ Fasting or chronic restrained eating.

What is considered 'normal' in terms of quantities and types of food consumed varies considerably from person to person. 'Normal eating' refers to the attitude a person holds in their relationship with food, rather than the type or amount of food they eat.

It is normal to:

⇨ Eat more on some days, less on others

⇨ Eat some foods just because they taste good

⇨ Have a positive attitude towards food

⇨ Not label foods with judgement words such as 'good', 'bad', 'clean'

⇨ Over-eat occasionally

⇨ Under-eat occasionally

⇨ Crave certain foods at times

⇨ Treat food and eating as one small part of a balanced life.

### Mindful eating

Mindful eating is a simple-to-learn life skill which can lead people to enjoy a satisfying, healthy and enjoyable relationship with food. It is a skill that can help people break free from 'food rules' and begin to enjoy healthy, flexible and relaxed eating practices. Mindful eating is not a diet. Mindful eating is about the way we eat, not what we eat.

## Dieting

Dieting is the number one risk factor in the development of an eating disorder.

Both the rate of obesity and the number of people with an eating disorder are increasing in Australia. Interestingly, the number of people with both obesity and an eating disorder has increased at a faster rate than the number of people with either obesity or an eating disorder alone. It has been suggested that these increasing numbers may be related to the proliferation of messages about the dangers of obesity, and behavioural responses to those messages that include people going on fad diets and engaging in both unhealthy and ineffective weight loss behaviours. The weight-loss industry in Australia is worth over $635 million, but it is clear that the methods used are rarely successful.

Research shows that women who diet severely are 18 times more likely to develop an eating disorder. Women who diet moderately are five times more likely to develop an eating disorder.

### Physical effects of dieting

The strict, restrictive and often unsustainable nature of many diets

can leave dieters feeling constantly hungry and deprived. Dieters often ignore this hunger for a short time but such deprivation can eventually lead to powerful food cravings and over-compensatory behaviour such as bingeing. This can in turn lead to feelings of shame and failure, which contribute to negative emotional associations with food and eating.

Fluctuating weight is common for people who diet frequently ('yo-yo' dieting), as most people regain all the weight they have lost after a diet within a few years.

Diets disconnect people from their natural bodily responses through imposed food related rules and restrictions which may overlook hunger, physical activity and a person's individual nutritional requirements.

Dieting can:

⇨ slow the body's metabolism (the rate it burns calories)

⇨ cause food cravings and an increased appetite, leading to over-eating

⇨ reduce the total amount of muscle tissue and bone density

⇨ cause constipation and/or diarrhoea

⇨ lower the body's temperature in order to use less energy

⇨ cause headaches

⇨ cause insomnia and fatigue

⇨ reduce the ability to feel hungry and full, making it easier to confuse hunger with emotional needs.

### Psychological effects of dieting

Dieting can lead to feelings of guilt over 'lack of self control', low self-esteem, a poor body image and obsessive thoughts and behaviours surrounding food. In addition, people who diet frequently are more likely to experience depression.

### Competitive dieting

Competitive dieting is a dangerous phenomenon which can lead to an obsession with food and weight obsession, as well as disordered eating behaviours. Television shows such as *The Biggest Loser* have seen a marked trend in competitive dieting programmes across many workplaces and gyms, whereby people are encouraged to participate individually or as teams to lose the most amount of weight in a specified time period, often for a prize or some form of reward.

Another example of competitive dieting can occur amongst secondary school students. In these instances, somebody may start a diet with friends and become obsessed with losing the most weight, leading to unhealthy and dangerous behaviours regarding food intake and/or physical activity levels. Competitive dieting may also occur in the context of physical activity, e.g. in sports. This can be equally as dangerous for the development of disordered eating or eating disorders, particularly amongst men.

# Chewing and Spitting (CHSP)

### What is chewing and spitting?

CHSP is a form of disordered eating where someone chews food, but spits it out rather than consuming it. Often the food is high in salt, sugar or fat, or regarded by the person as "bad" or "junk" food. Chewing the food for some time then spitting it out is seen as a way of enjoying the taste without gaining weight or consuming calories. CHSP can exist as a symptom of a diagnosed eating disorder, or as a separate form of disordered eating. CHSP is not widely recognised or researched, and people who engage in this behaviour can be reluctant to seek help due to guilt or shame.

## The physical effects of chewing and spitting

The sight, smell, thought and taste of food triggers the cephalic phase of gastric secretion which prepares the body for digesting food. Even though the food is not swallowed, CHSP triggers this response increasing stomach acids, digestive enzymes and insulin. When the food is not digested, the stomach acid can damage the stomach lining, causing ulcers. Insulin levels are also affected, which may potentially lead to weight gain and an altered metabolism.

Like bulimia, CHSP can also lead to dental problems such as tooth decay and cavities. Excessive chewing can also cause swollen salivary glands.

CHSP can lead to malnutrition if insufficient calories or nutrients are consumed. Many people who engage in chewing and spitting actually gain weight. This can be as a result of increased likelihood of binging on the "forbidden" foods, or unintentionally consuming extra calories. It may also be caused by the increase in insulin released into the body.

## Other effects of chewing and spitting

CHSP can be an addictive and uncontrollable behaviour that is very difficult to stop. It can lead to social isolation and feelings of guilt and shame.

It can also lead to financial difficulties due to the large quantities of food that are purchased but not consumed.

## Treatment

It is very important to get help for CHSP as it is a behaviour that can continue for many years and have severe health consequences. If you are in treatment for an eating disorder, make sure that your treatment team are aware that you are engaging in chewing and spitting. Contact the EDV Helpline on 1300 550 236, help@eatingdisorders.org.au or contact your local doctor as a first step.

## References

https://www.nationaleatingdisorders. org/blog/facts-about-chewing-and-spitting-disorder

https://jeatdisord.biomedcentral.com/articles/10.1186/s40337-016-0115-1

http://www.scienceofeds. org/2013/03/06/your-bodys-response-to-chewing-spitting-the-role-of-ghrelin-and-obestatin/

*21 February 2017*

⇨ The above information is reprinted with kind permission from Eating Disorders Victoria. Please visit www.eatingdisorders. org.au for further information.

# Overuse of fitness supplements could be a new eating disorder for men

## They're legal and over-the-counter, but is the way they're being used a good idea?

*By Jenn Savedge*

Much attention has been paid over the years to the way women perceive their bodies. But what about men? New research shines a spotlight on a growing trend among men to take supplements as a means to change the way they look – and asks whether or not the overuse of these supplements should be considered a new breed of eating disorder.

For decades women have been dealing with sexualized and Photoshopped images that send the message that to be thin is to be desirable. But now men are seeing more and more of these types of images of their own gender with an even more confusing message that promotes both a muscular and lean body type. To achieve this look, men are relying on shakes, pills and other "appearance or performance enhancing drugs" – or APEDs – that claim to foster the development of lean muscle mass.

In a new study, researchers took a closer look at the use of APEDs and asked whether their overuse is a new eating disorder for men.

For the study, researchers talked to about 200 men between the ages of 18 and 65 who worked out at least twice a week and also used fitness supplements such as whey protein, creatine and L-cartinine. The men were asked not only about their eating and exercise habits but also about their personal views about their bodies. Their results showed that many men use these supplements because they are unhappy with their physical appearance – a classic sign of an eating disorder.

Almost 30 per cent of the men surveyed were concerned about their AEPD use, yet, they continued to use them. Another bad sign. 40 per cent of men had increased their use of AEPDs over time and 22 per cent used these supplements to replace meals.

In the truly extreme cases, research found that eight per cent of the men had been advised by their doctor to cut back on their use of fitness supplements and three per cent had been hospitalised for kidney or liver problems after excessive use of AEPDs.

The report notes that AEPDs have become the primary means by which many men seek to change their bodies. While eating disorders in men are rarer and less talked about than those in women, researchers think this new tendency for men to use and abuse AEPDs as a means to a different body might be fostering a new strain of eating disorder in men – one that feeds on low-self esteem and is rooted in problems deeper than what can be solved at the gym.

To make matters worse, men are much less likely than women to even think about their habits in terms of an eating disorder. And if they do sense a problem, there are few resources available to men to help them address it.

The study's results were presented at the recent American Psychological Association meeting in Toronto where researchers debated the categorisation of the overuse of AEPD supplements as an eating disorder. Researchers hope that by shining a light on this issue, they can open up resources for men to help them address this growing problem.

*7 August 2015*

⇨ The above information is reprinted with kind permission from the Mother Nature Network. Please visit www.mnn.com for further information.

# 'Protorexia': can a protein-heavy diet become an unhealthy obsession?

## Why are you really using protein shakes?

*By Rachel Moss*

When eaten as part of a balanced diet, protein allows our body to grow and repair itself. But is there a risk of becoming obsessed with protein to the extent that behaviour becomes symptomatic of an eating disorder?

The term 'protorexia' has been coined to describe an unhealthy fixation with protein-heavy foods and supplements, such as protein shakes and chicken.

According to the numerous news outlets and bloggers writing on the subject, those suffering also tend to cut out foods they deem "unhealthy", such as carbs, in a bid to lose weight or build muscle.

The term has been linked to orthorexia – a condition defined as an "unhealthy obsession with healthy eating", which has yet to be formally recognised as an eating disorder.

According to eating disorders charity Beat, much like 'orthorexia', protorexia is not a recognised eating disorder and we should be careful how we are using the term. However, that doesn't mean people are not displaying concerning or unhealthy behaviours when it comes to consuming protein.

Speaking to The Huffington Post UK, a spokesperson from Beat said placing severe restrictions on diet "is obviously not healthy and may be an indication of an eating disorder".

"But it's important to remember that eating disorders are not really about food itself but about thoughts and feelings," they added.

"A sufferer's treatment of food, whether restricting, bingeing, purging, or any combination of these, may be about coping with these thoughts and feelings, or a way to feel in control.

"It's entirely possible that someone might use clean eating or protein shakes in this way, but protorexia is not a clinical diagnosis."

Despite this there are studies to suggest many are experiencing an unhealthy or obsessive relationship with protein.

A 2015 study by Dr Richard Achiro and Dr Peter Theodore found that many men who use protein powder to build muscle feel similar psychological pressure to people who've been diagnosed with recognised eating disorders.

In the study of almost 200 men who use the powders, 29% said they were worried by their supplement intake, while a further 8% admitted they'd been advised to reduce their use by a medical professional.

The study suggested body-conscious individuals often began consuming high levels of protein believing those with ripped torsos must be "healthy", without realising the internal impact this may cause.

But how can you recognise if your gym buddy is using protein shakes to simply improve their workout or if they're part of a more serious, underlying issue?

According to Beat, it's common to believe you can "see" an eating disorder, but they are mental illnesses, and psychological and behavioural signs are likely to emerge long before physical ones.

"Secretiveness around or preoccupation with food, becoming withdrawn, mood swings, low self-esteem, tiredness, and distorted perceptions of weight are some of the signs that someone might be developing some form of eating disorder," the spokesperson said.

"Beat has recently launched a campaign to help people recognise the early signs of eating disorders."

Writing for *Women's Health*, Sarah Shephard identified as a 'protorexic' and said she initially upped her protein intake to enhance her workouts, but things soon got out of hand.

"At first I found that a shake post workout upped my stamina and annulled my hunger," she said.

"So I started subbing one in for breakfast and as I became more interested in how protein could fuel my workout – and the inevitable flipside: how carbs could be hindering my results – every meal became based around it. An inevitable part of the process was that carbs became all but banished from my diet."

Shephard soon began to struggle to focus at work and constantly felt too tired to socialise with friends. Thankfully, she visited a nutritionist who explained her restrictive diet was to blame and helped her reintroduce balance to her life.

Nutritionist and British Dietetic Association spokesperson Chloe Miles told HuffPost UK by focusing on consuming a lot of one nutrient, such as protein, you are likely to be restricting other food groups such as carbohydrates.

"This may lead to you missing out on other important parts of a diet, such as fibre," she said.

"Fibre is found in fruit, vegetables and wholegrains and is really important for a healthy digestive system."

She explained that protein may fill someone up so much that they are "unable to eat enough of the other things we need in our diet".

"Animal protein, often, contains saturated fat, so if people are increasing their protein intake using animal protein it may be detrimental to heart health, by increasing their intake of saturated fat," she said.

"There are risks of having an unbalanced diet including vitamin and mineral deficiencies and in the long term increasing the risk of developing chronic conditions."

According to Beat, anyone concerned that they or someone they know may be developing an eating disorder should "access treatment as quickly as possible, as this ensures the best chance of recovery".

"The first port of call is usually your GP, who should ideally refer you for assessment by an eating disorders specialist," they said.

"Beat has produced literature to help sufferers, those supporting them, and GPs during the appointment to help get a positive outcome here.

"And of course the Beat helpline is also available every day from 4pm–10pm on 0808 801 0677 or at help@b-eat.co.uk for anyone who is worried about themselves or someone they know."

While it's important to be mindful of our protein intake and take any potential signs of any eating disorder seriously, nutrition consultant Charlotte Stirling-Reed confirmed that we should not fear protein.

"Protein is one of the building blocks of life and therefore is an important macronutrient to include in your diet every day," she told HuffPost UK.

"Most of us get enough protein by eating a well-balanced diet and varying the foods we eat every day, so there is no need to worry too much about getting enough.

"Including two to three protein-rich foods such as lentils, nuts, beans, meat or fish every day is what the government recommends for good health."

*28 February 2017*

⇨ The above information is reprinted with kind permission from The Huffington Post UK. Please visit www.huffingtonpost.co.uk for further information.

# Clean eating trend can be dangerous for young people, experts warn

*Mental health specialists say following ultra-healthy diets could have negative impact on people at risk of eating disorders.*

*By Sarah Marsh and Denis Campbell*

Mental health experts are warning of the risks of the increasingly popular 'clean eating' dietary trend, which is leaving a growing number of teenagers very thin and even at risk of dying when taken to extremes.

One nutritionist said she had been contacted by a girl as young as 12 and people had got in touch on social media saying they wanted to be healthier, giving details of their existing diets.

Rhiannon Lambert, a registered associate nutritionist in Harley Street, London, has encountered people who obsess over where food comes from and some clients who will not drink water from a tap, because they normally stick to a brand of bottled water.

"They develop particular habits, or won't eat food when walking, because they think that food can only be processed when they're sitting down," she said. "All this interferes with general life and becomes an obsession."

Lambert, who treats about 180 clients a year with various kinds of eating disorders, says has seen the number of those presenting due to 'clean eating' double in the last year.

The extreme form of this is a psychological condition known as orthorexia nervosa, the Californian doctor Steven Bratman has said. Experts have described it as a "fixation with righteous eating".

Clean eating is promoted by some food bloggers, who are increasingly felt by a number of medical experts to be having a negative impact on certain vulnerable young people.

"Young people lose sleep over this and cannot afford the lifestyle needed to maintain it," Lambert said. "Health

> "My problem with the word clean is that it has become too complicated. It has become too loaded.
>
> "When I first read the term, it meant natural, unprocessed. Now it doesn't mean that at all. It means diet. It means fad."
>
> Deliciously Ella, 'Horizon: Clean Eating – The Dirty Truth', BBC

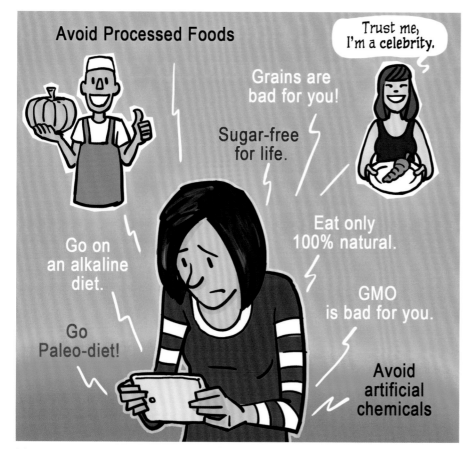

bloggers can be unqualified and offer dangerous advice. Not all of them want to impose their lifestyle on others, but lots of them do and they often give advice on clean eating with no scientific backing.

"The books come along, the products come along and these people are now role models whose every word will inspire impressionable young people. I have clients who think they have to be vegan to be successful."

There are no official figures for the number of children and young people following a clean eating regime, because orthorexia is not recognised as a clinical diagnosis. But psychologists and nutritionists have reported a recent surge in the phenomenon among younger clients, especially girls, and believe that it is gaining in popularity.

The eating disorders charity Beat told *The Guardian* that it had recently seen a rise in the number of calls to its helpline from young people who have experienced problems as a result of following the trend.

Ursula Philpot, a dietitian at the British Dietetic Association, said a fixation with eating healthily had been a noticeable route into eating disorders

for vulnerable individuals in the past couple of years.

She identified social media and the rise of healthy food trends and blogs as key drivers of the trend, but said it is difficult to blame them completely. "If it wasn't health bloggers, then it could be something else that becomes the inroad, but it seems to be the route in now," she said.

Orthorexia affects girls more than boys, although boys are much more affected than previously, she added.

The range of foods that people worry about eating has changed, Philpot said. "At the top of most people's lists [of bad foods] is gluten and dairy. When you talk to young people more, you find out about their stringent rules – some will worry all day about eating a biscuit," she said.

The condition starts out as an innocent attempt to eat more healthily, but those who experience it become fixated on food quality and purity, according to experts.

A Beat spokeswoman said: "We are concerned by the rising trend of 'clean eating' and the impact it could have on young people vulnerable to the development of an eating disorder. We are aware that contacts to our helpline

are raising issues around orthorexia and clean eating."

There may be several reasons for someone to take up clean eating, the spokeswoman said.

"Eating disorders are serious mental illnesses and their causes are many and complex. Research is telling us that they may be more biologically based than we previously thought, but social and environmental factors will also play a part in their development," she said.

"Orthorexia does not have a clinical diagnosis and it would be for clinicians to determine whether it should, which may be helpful, because then it would have a clear clinical pathway of treatment.

"There is a view that it may be more closely connected to OCD due to the nature of the illness, although it does also share behavioural traits with anorexia. Anorexia has the highest mortality rate of any mental illness."

Deanne Jade, the founder of the National Centre for Eating Disorders, a counselling network, said the number of cases of orthorexia that she dealt with had more than doubled over the last five years.

She said: "A lot of younger people don't think they need therapy and that the solution to bulimia and anorexia is to eat clean, but this can become an obsession and there's now more pressure than ever to be healthy.

"There are too many messages in the media and especially social media. What worries me is that a lot of people promoting these ideas have no knowledge of nutrition.

"I don't know what the solution is, but a lot of the time getting people to recover from an eating disorder means getting them to relax their ideas about clean eating."

*1 October 2016*

⇨ The above information is reprinted with kind permission from *The Guardian*. Please visit www.theguardian.com for further information.

# A dietitian puts extreme 'clean eating' claims to the test – and the results aren't pretty

*An article from* **The Conversation.**

*By Sophie Medlin, Lecturer in Nutrition and Dietetics, King's College London*

THE CONVERSATION

"Clean eating" is associated with the healthy lifestyle and body beautiful that is promoted by many online bloggers. While the term is heavily used in social media, there has never been any agreement on what it really means or any comprehensive studies examining the potential benefits of a clean eating lifestyle as a whole.

However, the core principles that the big names in this movement champion appear to be: eliminate processed food; reduce salt intake; eat more vegetables; choose whole grains; eliminate refined sugar; reduce alcohol. For some, you also need to be gluten, dairy, and soya free and to eat raw (depending on how militant you are, food has to be entirely uncooked or only mildly heated). And if you want to be completely "clean" you should probably be vegan, too. Quite a list, then.

And there are also some big players online – including Food Babe, who was voted by *Time Magazine* as one of the 30 most influential people on the Internet – who have significantly influenced this trend.

While some of the principles of clean eating are in line with the best available evidence for losing weight or preventing ill health – such as eating plenty of fruit and vegetables, sticking to wholegrains and limiting processed food – there are plenty of others that don't stand up to scrutiny. It has been repeatedly proven that dietary restrictions such as a dairy-free diet or gluten-free diet are nutritionally substandard and studies have linked the introduction of a gluten-free diet with increased levels of psychological distress in coeliacs, including depression and anxiety.

Some people find it difficult to understand why dietitians and doctors are against the clean eating phenomenon when there are still people eating burgers for breakfast and obesity is on the rise. However, some clean eating is sensationalist promotion of non-evidence-based, and extremely restrictive, lifestyles that demonise everyday food essentials. And that can lead followers into having a sense of shame and failure for not eliminating "unclean" foods 100% of the time – so you can see where the negativity from healthcare professionals stems from.

There is significant research disproving many of the principles of the diet. Below are some of the big claims and why they don't stack up.

### Clean eating can cure disease

Some clean eating bloggers claim to have cured themselves of diseases. The kinds of medical conditions that clean eating is supposed to cure are often conditions that are not well understood, such as chronic fatigue, which leaves sufferers desperate for a solution. And where there is desperation there is always someone willing to sell help – however unscientific.

One of the big names in clean eating who believes her diet controls her Postural Tachycardia Syndrome – where standing up causes a drop in blood supply to the heart and brain and the heart races to compensate – intestinal issues and headaches through her method of a dairy free, gluten free vegan diet is Deliciously Ella. PoTS, however, has no proven link with food except that a higher salt intake is recommended to help keep blood pressure up. Having too little salt in the diet can exacerbate the problem. The reason that Ella is so much better now is much more likely to be age-related as we know that for 80% of sufferers, symptoms disappear between the ages of 19–24. Ella was diagnosed aged 19 in 2011 and has been blogging about diet for four years.

One thing diet may have helped with though is Ella's gastrointestinal issues. Her method of eating has a diet that is very low in fermentable carbohydrates, or FODMAPs, which have been robustly proven to be a cause of Irritable Bowel Syndrome (IBS) which affects up to one in five people.

### Clean eating makes you happy!

Many of the clean eating bloggers promote themselves as a model of how you could look if you follow their lifestyle. But it is important to remember that it is their job to look the way they do. If you have a full-time job and a busy life, the chances of you cooking every meal from scratch, never having to grab a sandwich from the supermarket for lunch and being able to work out for two hours a day are very slim. If you try to model your life on theirs you are more than likely to end up feeling like a failure because it is simply not realistic.

Interestingly, many clean eating bloggers claim to have been depressed before clean eating. There has been lots of research into dietary treatments for depression by increasing an amino acid called tryptophan which is a precursor for serotonin production in the brain, which in turn influences good mood. To date, no trial has conclusively proven that increasing dietary tryptophan improves serotonin production or depressive symptoms but a diet in line with clean eating actually has the potential to be low in essential amino acids such as tryptophan.

What is more likely is that all the attention and apparent public approval received for losing weight and improving their appearance has temporarily improved their self-worth.

## Clean eating is a good way to lose weight

Clean Eating Alice, 23, is another big name in the game. Alice isn't vegetarian but her diet is very low in carbohydrate. She claims that her diet and exercise regime has immeasurably improved her health and happiness. It was reported that through her version of clean eating and intensive exercise, she dropped 2st 7lb (16kg) and reduced her body fat percentage from 30% to just 15%.

Alice's reported body fat percentage is concerning. The minimum essential fat for a woman is between ten to 13% – we need this amount to maintain our immune system and maintain healthy hormone levels. Many professional athletes will have a body fat percentage of up to 20% with the normal healthy level around 25%. So holding herself up as a realistic and achievable role model is highly misleading.

## Clean eating is good for gut health

The Helmsley Sisters were some of the first to bring the clean eating trend to our attention. Their philosophy aims to help people with their digestion and relationship with food, and teach the importance of gut health. Their recipes eliminate gluten, grains and refined sugar (and minimise natural sugars).

However, the majority of people tolerate gluten very well – the exceptions are for people with conditions such as coeliac disease – sugar is absorbed so efficiently it has no impact on digestion and grains provide high levels of prebiotics to feed the good bacteria in your gut. The best thing for gut health is a good, balanced diet.

## Clean eating prevents ageing

Many bloggers state that clean eating will keep you looking youthful. There is some compelling evidence that antioxidants found in fruit and vegetables can prevent premature skin ageing.

You do, however, also need plenty of good quality protein to maintain the integrity of your skin and therefore extreme clean eating could easily undermine the benefits of the antioxidants.

## Clean eating will detox your body

Detox diets are all the rage and the clean eating crew all have their own version of a detox diet. Fortunately, no one needs a detox diet because our liver and our kidneys are always already doing this. Everyone would agree that excessive consumption of highly processed food with lots of additives is not a healthy way to eat. However, neither is following a highly restrictive diet for any amount of time and there is certainly no health benefits associated with 'detoxing'.

Some clean eaters promote an alkaline diet to prevent excess acidity in the body. Ironically, our stomach acid is only slightly less acidic than battery acid so anything you eat will be immediately placed into a highly acidic environment where the pH is tightly controlled. You cannot manipulate your body's pH through diet and you don't need to try.

## Clean eating makes you healthier

There are even more extreme examples of clean eating out there including Freelee The Banana Girl who promotes a raw vegan diet of 15 bananas, 40 pieces of fruit and a couple of kilograms of potatoes a day. She claims that eating this way has cured her weight issues, depression, irritable bowel syndrome, chronic fatigue, poor digestion and acne.

It is hard to pin down the most concerning thing about this diet but the fact that Freelee is consuming 6.5 times more potassium than is recommended and encourages others to do so is a

big one. She even consumes 30% more potassium than is shown to cause excess potassium in the blood, which can lead to deadly changes in heart rhythm. That said, whether or not she is absorbing any of the nutrients in her food due to the amount of fibre she is taking in is questionable and if her bowel habits are normal and healthy it is a medical miracle.

Anyone can call themselves a nutritionist and there are many quick courses that give a false air of credibility. There are also no regulations around what people can and can't recommend as being healthy. It should be very hard to maintain a voice of authority in an area in which you are totally unqualified and in a world where your self-worth depends on 'likes' and 'views' and 'followers'.

An obsession with clean eating and the shame that is often associated with eating foods considered to be dirty can also lead to mental health issues such as orthorexia, an eating disorder associated with obsessive healthy eating. Emmy Gilmore, clinical director of eating disorders clinic Recover, even suggested in a recent BBC documentary that many UK clean eating bloggers had sought help from her clinic. So rather than watch videos of supposedly physically healthy girls as gospel, it's better to develop healthy eating habits that come from sound scientific advice and which balance all the nutrients your body needs.

And if you're seeking professional advice, find a nutritionist with a degree or a registered dietitian – it's a protected title so you can be certain that the advice you're given will be scientifically robust.

*8 September 2016*

⇨  The above information is reprinted with kind permission from *The Conversation*. Please visit www. theconversation.com for further information.

# 'Fox & Moon' diet planners may "exacerbate eating disorders", charity warns

### One diary says: "Stop rewarding yourself with food, you are not a dog."

*By Rachel Moss*

A stationery company has been accused of fuelling eating disorders through the controversial slogans on its food diaries and diet planners.

UK-based Fox & Moon sells diaries covered with phrases such as "I want to skinny dip not chunky dunk" and "stop rewarding yourself with food, you are not a dog".

On Twitter, some have called the diaries "dangerous" while others have labelled them "eating disorder propaganda".

The UK's leading eating disorders charity, Beat, told HuffPost UK the diaries may "exacerbate the illness in those who are already suffering or vulnerable".

Blogger Lottie L'amour was among the first to tweet about the planners after seeing a diary on Instagram reading: "Do it for the 'holy shit you got hot'."

"For people struggling with eating disorders, phrases like this can be really damaging," she told metro.co.uk.

"I don't think they realise that words like this can trigger damaging eating habits that can lead to serious health problems and death in some cases."

Commenting on the backlash, a spokesperson from Beat said: "Eating disorders are serious mental illnesses with very complex causes and it's important that this isn't trivialised.

"It is unlikely that this kind of messaging would be the sole and direct cause of an eating disorder.

"However, it may exacerbate the illness in those who are already suffering or vulnerable."

But others have argued the planners are just a bit of fun.

*15 May 2017*

⇨ The above information is reprinted with kind permission from The Huffington Post UK. Please visit www.huffingtonpost.co.uk for further information.

---

# It's not a teenage thing – women in their 40s or 50s suffer from eating disorders too

### Traumas during childhood and personality traits increase risk of developing eating disorders well into adulthood.

*By Lea Surugue*

It is not just teenage girls who suffer from eating disorders: in the UK, roughly 3.6% of women in their 40s and 50s could also be affected. A number of risk factors, such as the death of a parent or sexual abuse in childhood, may make it more likely for women of this age to report an eating disorder diagnosis.

Eating disorders are severe psychiatric issues associated with major health consequences and high levels of mortality. They are described in the *Diagnostic and Statistical Manual for Mental Disorders* 5th edition (DSM-5) and range from anorexia nervosa and bulimia to binge-eating disorder and purging disorder.

These disorders frequently appear in adolescence and are more common among young people – girls in particular. According to the charity Anorexia and Bulimia Care, anorexia most commonly develops around the age of 16 or 17, while bulimia mainly affects females aged between 16 and 40.

However, eating disorder cases can also be diagnosed well into adulthood and among young children. Research into eating disorders is thus expanding to take into account this complex reality, and to help doctors improve how they treat these conditions.

The latest study on the topic, published in *BMC Medicine,* is the first to look at the prevalence of eating disorders among women in their fourth or fifth decade of life. The scientists wanted to find out what proportion of women at this age had been diagnosed with an eating disorder in the last 12 months or at any other point in their lives. Looking back at the women's life experiences, they also analysed what risk factors made such a diagnosis more likely.

### Affecting 3% of women

The researchers, led by Dr Nadia Micali from Icahn School of Medicine at Mount Sinai and University College London, collected data from women taking part in the Avon Longitudinal Study of Parents and Children. This extensive, population-based prospective study of UK women and their children investigates the effects of environment, genetic and other factors on health and development.

Some 5, 658 of these women filled in

a questionnaire where they recorded if they had experienced symptoms of eating disorders sometime during their lifetime. The women were 47 years old, on average.

Some 524 women who had symptoms of a disorder and 518 who didn't were together selected to go through standardised diagnostic interviews to confirm a diagnosis. This allowed the scientists to estimate the prevalence of these conditions among these older women. Around 15.3% of participants were found to have had an eating disorder at some point in their lives, and 3.6% in the past 12 months. Among these, nearly half of them were diagnosed for the first time.

"Our study challenges the view that developing eating disorders is something that happens to adolescents and young adults. Women in their 40s and 50s are also affected. However, it is difficult to say whether this is a new phenomenon or if it is because we had not studied this age group before", Micali told IBTimes UK.

## Trauma in childhood

The scientists also conducted interviews to learn more about the women's childhoods and life experiences. In particular, they looked at whether factors such as childhood happiness, early sexual abuse, parental deaths or separation, interpersonal sensitivity (the ability to accurately assess other people's feelings) and IQ scores increased the risk of developing an eating disorder.

Although none of these factors is enough on its own to trigger the development of eating disorders, the scientists showed that parental separation or divorce in childhood was associated with increased odds for bulimia, binge-eating disorder and atypical anorexia.

Sexual abuse in childhood was associated with binge-eating behaviours, and the death of a parent with seven-fold increased odds for purging disorder. Women who rated their childhood as unhappy were more likely to report any of these four eating disorders: they had increased by 4-10% per unit score of 'unhappiness' of developing anorexia and bulimia if they reported being unhappy when young.

Higher interpersonal sensitivity was associated with an increased risk of binge eating by 19% per unit score of 'sensitivity'.

"All these factors are important because they are preventable or, at the very least, if we know about them we can offer support and therapy to people to try and help them before they go on to develop eating disorders," Micali said.

Despite the relatively high prevalence of these disorders at mid-life and the fact they are sometimes linked to important childhood traumas, very few women told the researchers that they had sought or received treatment. Improving access to care at all ages of life and researching in greater details the long-term impact of childhood traumas will be very important in years to come to reduce the incidence of eating disorders.

*17 January 2017*

⇨ The above information is reprinted with kind permission from the *International Business Times*. Please visit www.ibtimes.co.uk for further information.

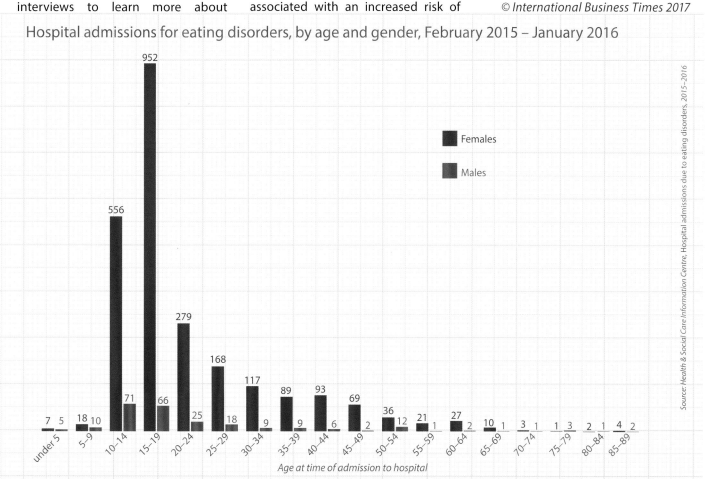

Hospital admissions for eating disorders, by age and gender, February 2015 – January 2016

*Age at time of admission to hospital*

Source: Health & Social Care Information Centre, Hospital admissions due to eating disorders, 2015–2016

# Eating disorders in men rise by 70% in NHS figures

**Number of men admitted to hospital with eating disorder grew at same rate as among women between 2010 and 2016.**

*By Sarah Marsh*

The number of adult men being admitted to hospital with an eating disorder has risen by 70% over the past six years – the same rate of increase as among women.

NHS Digital data analysed by *The Guardian* shows the number of hospital diagnoses in male over-19s rose from 480 in 2010–2011 to 818 between April 2015 and March 2016.

The rate of increase was slightly higher among older men, at 70% for the 41–60 age group, compared with 67% in the 26–40 category and 63% among 19- to 25-year-olds. In the same period, there was a 61% increase among women aged 19 to 25 and a 76% rise among middle-aged women.

The figures come after it was revealed that steroid use among young people quadrupled in the past year. The Home Office's crime survey found the biggest rise in anabolic steroid use was among 16- to 24-year-olds, with an extra 19,000 taking the drug.

Medical leaders and health experts have put the growing numbers down to pressure from popular culture and social media. But more awareness about eating disorders may be encouraging life-long sufferers to come forward and talk about their problems, they believe.

Dr William Rhys Jones, of the Royal College of Psychiatrists' eating disorders faculty, said: "Pressure for body perfection is on the rise for men of all ages, which is a risk factor for developing an eating disorder. Images of unhealthy male body ideals in the media place unnecessary pressure on vulnerable people who strive for acceptance through the way they look."

He said a continued lack of understanding and sometimes sympathy for men suffering from eating disorders remained a barrier for some who needed help. "We must continue to address the ongoing gender bias around eating disorders so every man who is suffering feels comfortable to get help when they need it."

Prof Helen Stokes-Lampard, chair of the Royal College of GPs, said the rise was not surprising "when you consider the unrelenting pressures placed on people by popular culture and social media".

She called for schools, universities and employers to be more aware of the danger signs. "[These] can include excessive dieting or daily trips to the gym, eating large amounts of food, the inappropriate use of laxatives and obsessions around weight and appearance," she said.

Stokes-Lampard said there was a growing awareness that eating disorders affected both men and women. "Increased awareness among sufferers and health professionals has likely meant that men are starting to recognise their symptoms more and are being diagnosed more, meaning that they are more likely to be referred to eating disorders services," she said.

The eating disorder charity Beat said increases in hospital admissions may be a positive sign. Tom Quinn, its director of external affairs, said: "It's possible [the increase] indicates an increasing awareness that these illnesses affect people regardless of gender."

Earlier diagnosis and treatment would lower the chance of an illness developing to the point when they required hospital treatment, he added. "There is still a long way to go to ensure that all sufferers get the treatment they need as quickly as possible."

Figures released last year showed people with eating disorders in England could wait for up to 182 days for treatment. Patients surveyed by Beat expressed concern about GPs who were failing to refer people for specialist assistance. Half of those with some experience of an eating disorder rated GP care as poor or very poor, and 30% said they were not referred to mental health services after their appointment.

Sam Thomas, the founder of the charity Men Get Eating Disorders Too, said the UK had no dedicated

| Hospital admissions by gender from 10–24 years old for an eating disorder, Feb 2015– Jan 2016 | | |
|---|---|---|
| Age | Female | Male |
| 10 | 14 | 2 |
| 11 | 32 | 10 |
| 12 | 81 | 9 |
| 13 | 161 | 24 |
| 14 | 268 | 26 |
| 15 | 308 | 29 |
| 16 | 253 | 21 |
| 17 | 196 | 9 |
| 18 | 114 | 1 |
| 19 | 81 | 6 |
| 20 | 79 | 5 |
| 21 | 71 | 4 |
| 22 | 45 | 9 |
| 23 | 38 | 3 |
| 24 | 46 | 4 |

*Source: Health & Social Care Information Centre, Hospital admissions due to eating disorders, 2015–2016*

facilities for male patients. "Usually places will have two separate rooms they prioritise for men but that can reinforce any sense of isolation, and eating disorders thrive on that," he said. "Some services literally cannot admit men. One guy I know has been waiting months and months. He has had a heart attack and is desperately unwell and he is still waiting for a referral. He is on about seven waiting lists."

Data shows that men still account for a small proportion of the total patients diagnosed in hospital, with 1,098 male adults and children admitted in 2015–16 and 12,054 female adults and children. More than 300 boys and girls aged 12 or under were admitted to hospital with an eating disorder in 2015–16.

The fastest rate of change among all ages over the six-year period was in 13- to 15-year-olds. Diagnosis numbers over the period more than doubled, from 565 to 1,383.

Rhiannon Lambert, a Harley Street nutritionist, said: "One key marker between men and women is that women tend to be more honest in their symptoms whereas men typically suggest they are on a physique transformation journey.

"There is a stereotype that eating disorders still only apply to privileged, appearance-obsessed women. This huge misconception exists which pushes the harmful notion that a great many others are not at risk. I have met people of every race, gender, sexuality and personality with disordered eating patterns. Eating disorders do not discriminate, they are a complex mental health illness that can affect everyone."

## Case study: Dave Chawner, 28, from London

When I was 17, I got a role in a play and I had to appear topless. It was the only time I had ever really thought about my body and so I lost a bit of weight. People started saying "you look good" and that made me feel great. Losing weight gave me approval and meant "being good" in my mind.

It came at a time when I had a lot of other stuff going on – including applications, exams and deadlines.

Everything felt intense and my grades were not good but losing weight was.

Eventually the people around me picked up on it, and took me aside for a quiet word. But I didn't acknowledge I had a problem. It was only when I was 21 that I first said that I had anorexia. I got a job over the summer in a boarding school which was completely catered for. It really affected me how little control I had over the food. I started exercising during the night, binging and purging. One of the teachers, who had experienced bulimia herself, asked me if I was anorexic. I thought: "I do have anorexia."

At my worst I was weighing myself four or five times a day, coffee loading, exercising during the night. I would have mood swings and constantly feel thirsty because when you're not eating your brain thinks you must need a drink. I was also constantly freezing.

Over the years, it faded in and out of prevalence. How bad things were depended on how much I wanted to escape life and numb myself. I am a comedian and I started doing shows about my illness when I was about 23. It went better than I thought but people said "you don't look anorexic" and that made me feel like a fraud. So I had a relapse and ended up needing outpatient treatment at the Maudsley Hospital in London. I was treated there for two-and-a-half-years and finished therapy about three or four months ago. I found it really helpful.

It is still an open book in terms of what will happen in terms of my eating disorder, but I feel the furthest away from anorexia that I ever have.

As a man, I never found it hard to get help because I am very open and can talk about what is going on. I could go to my GP and explain what was on my mind and they did take me seriously. I know not everyone can be so open.

Although it's awful to see more men suffering from eating disorders it's great that more are having the balls to stand up and come forward, saying

they don't feel stigma anymore. If a man came into the doctor with cancer or heart disease, would we treat them differently to a woman? It's easy to create a barrier that doesn't need to be there.

I think it's lazy to blame social media for the rise in eating disorders – they existed before Facebook. However, now it's like people have someone looking over their shoulder as everything is documented. It's not helpful that people Photoshop their photos and present an unrealistic image to the world that is unobtainable.

Having an eating disorder is like a constant background noise, a hum that is never completely there but also never ever taken away. It's not that I didn't like food. I was always thinking about how I could eat and feel full without having any calories. It is like being an alcoholic, it's not something that ever goes away. It's a kind of colour to your existence but it makes life so unstable.

For hundreds of thousands anorexia isn't sexy, interesting or exciting – it's just a shit, boring, mundane, anxiety-ridden hell for them. I am trying to help make that clear, to present a more authentic portrayal of it.

*31 July 2017*

⇨ The above information is reprinted with kind permission from *The Guardian*. Please visit www.theguardian.com for further information.

# A new way to teach children about eating disorders

THE CONVERSATION

*An article from* **The Conversation.**

*By Emma Rich, Reader, Department for Health, University of Bath; Niamh Ni Shuilleabhain, PhD Researcher in the Department for Health, University of Bath; Simone Fullagar Professor, Sport and Physical Cultural Studies, University of Bath*

An estimated 1.6 million people in the UK have experienced an eating disorder. In the US, these figures are as high as 20 million women and 10 million men. With numbers like these, and rising levels of body disaffection among young people, tackling eating disorders is an increasingly urgent task.

As well as leading to potentially life-threatening conditions, eating disorders have significant social and economic impacts. While we are often told of the burden of obesity on the NHS, it is also worth remembering that eating disorders are reported to cost the British economy £15 billion each year.

These figures are a powerful reminder of the futility of single solutions to complex health problems. The influential (but sometimes simple) approach that focuses on a response to the cult of slenderness, body image and the role of the media, has had a powerful impact on the programmes developed in schools. But eating disorders are extremely complicated conditions. To address this, we are undertaking a collaborative research project with the charity Anorexia and Bulimia Care to explore a more comprehensive approach.

Dealing with the psychological concept of 'body image' for example, often focuses on teaching strategies to control an individual's attitudes in response to external pressures such as media images and peer pressure (both online and offline). The argument goes that eating disorders are linked to the negative body images that develop as a result of the "cult of slenderness" in contemporary media.

While media imagery plays a part, focusing only on body image may be limiting. It fails to tackle the broader socio-cultural conditions within which body disaffection and eating disorders flourish. There is a need to recognise the limitations of a young person's individual agency in the context of competing messages about healthy bodies that stir up emotions of fear, shame and disgust. Within popular culture, but also, crucially, within official health policy, bodies worthy of aspiration are thin, fit and desirable. They are certainly not "big".

It may be time to move towards a health education about healthy bodies within a broader context that challenges body size as the focal point of health. *The Fat Pedagogy Reader* is a publication that supports building a more fat-positive system of education. The research reveals that exploration of complex social environments should be as central to these programmes as weight, food and the media.

Because while body image, size and weight are certainly important factors, disordered eating and disaffection may equally be about issues of power and control. Research elsewhere points to a wide range of struggles for recognition that young people experience both within and beyond school boundaries. Yet the focus on the culture of slenderness and body image still occupies the focus of many education programmes designed to address body disaffection.

There is a real need for programmes to move beyond a focus on the individual and the perils of the media. We should be

Anti-Social Media
Puerile Press
Mindless Television
Trash Magazines

working towards a more sophisticated understanding of how culture, injustice and distress are experienced through young people's bodies and eating practices.

## A difficult subject

It is not sufficient or realistic to simply attempt to adjust the mindset of an individual through short-term intervention, and expect large scale, lasting change. In order to reduce the incidence of eating disorders and body disaffection in schools, a change is needed in the broader environment of school culture. This includes the attitudes of popular culture, parents, health promotion, sport and arts, and mental health services. This will enable moving beyond oppositional thinking about a body's identity as simply fat or thin, healthy or unhealthy, and success or failure.

In the meantime it is important to recognise that current programmes in this area are well intentioned, and not without merit. Teachers may feel torn between what are seen as competing health agendas. Schools are being positioned as vehicles through which to address a range of health problems, on the one hand the concerns about the rise in childhood obesity and on the other, rising levels of unhealthy weight loss.

Although eating disorders and obesity are part of a bigger picture of complex experiences, too often they are seen as having competing agendas and can leave teachers unsure of how best to address sensitive issues related to weight and the body. Current approaches are failing to address and challenge the stigma and stereotypes surrounding the concept of "being fat". Failing to engage with the complex discourses that shape how children come to learn about the body and health risks fuelling bullying and perpetuating misinformed practices surrounding weight control in schools.

*1 March 2017*

⇨ The above information is reprinted with kind permission from *The Conversation*. Please visit www.theconversation.com for further information.

© 2010–2017,
*The Conversation Trust (UK)*

# Tackling the challenge of exercise during recovery from an eating disorder

The issue of exercise can cause a lot of worry and uncertainty when an individual is recovering from an eating disorder. Over-exercising is often a feature of anorexia, carried out compulsively as a tool in weight loss and maintenance of the disorder.

Eating disorder inpatient units provide an environment where exercise is very precisely managed. Zero exercise will be allowed at low weight and further into treatment when exercise is slowly introduced, it will be gentle and carefully managed activity. At Newbridge, young people join Leisure Group, which enables them to do yoga, moving on to badminton and finally swimming (undertaken in conjunction with body image work).

However, once a young person leaves the inpatient unit and returns home, it isn't possible to control exercise in the same way. So how should reintroduction to exercise be managed?

"This is something parents are very concerned about as they prepare for discharge," explains Gill Williams, Newbridge nurse who runs the Programme for Parents. "We advise it is much better for young people to take up organised activities and team sports, because these are structured activities within specific time frames and there are social benefits in being part of a team or group." The structured nature of team practices and organised activities make it more feasible to plan and agree additional snacks to compensate for energy used and to ensure exercise is contained within clear limits.

"We would be much more concerned about a young person in recovery going running alone," explains Gill. "There is the risk of runs getting longer and more frequent and no benefits of socialising with others." If a young person prefers going to the gym to team sports, see if you can join them at the gym so their exercise is not a lone activity without time limits.

Normally, it is the compulsive approach to exercise which may still need to be considered and after discharge. "Think about the motivation an individual has for exercising," explains Sue Taylor, HCA, who also works on the Programme for Parents. "Your daughter or son might say – 'It makes me feel better'. This is exactly the role of sports and exercise for many, many people. But if the individual feels bad and guilty and bad if they don't exercise, that is an indication they still have a problematic relationship with exercise."

All sports and activities are not the same in terms of risk for individuals in recovery from an eating disorder. Endurance sports such as long distance running and triathlons present a raised risk because of the very high levels of energy and dedication they demand (and how this can be expressed in a person predisposed to eating disorders). Aesthetic sports such as dancing and ice skating are higher risk for young people in recovery because of their potential to maintain body image anxiety.

But it is widely agreed that even though exercise presents challenges for the recovering anorexic, it isn't possible or advisable for individuals to permanently avoid exercise. "Often, sport and exercise is a big part of young people's lives before they became ill," explains Sue. "Sport and exercise became a tool of anorexia while they were ill, but in recovery, young people are often very keen to enjoy exercising again."

If the route back into exercise is a positive one, such as someone taking up a team sport and finding a function for exercise which is primarily about enjoyment, socialising and belonging, this can be supportive of recovery," says Gill. "We know how important motivation is in the process of recovery; building up a full life which they don't want to lose by becoming ill again. Safe, balanced exercise as part of a team or an enjoyable regular activity can serve as important motivation to maintain recovery."

⇨ The above information is reprinted with kind permission from Newbridge House. Please visit www.newbridge-health.org.uk.

© *Newbridge House 2017*

# How I manage my eating disorder

**An extra from A grown-up approach to treating anorexia.**

Carrie Arnold endured more than a decade of anorexia before finding a way to understand it that helped her loosen its grip on her life.

"When I was first diagnosed with anorexia more than 15 years ago, no one told me anything about biology or neuroscience or genetics. The reason I continued to starve myself despite my failing organs and being forced to drop out of school, they said, was that something was wrong in my family. And as soon as that was sorted out, my eating disorder would be out of a job and I would get well. One therapist told me my parents were too controlling. Another said that there was too much pressure on me to be perfect. Yet another suggested that I just didn't want to grow up, and my mother was afraid to let me leave the nest.

"The problem was that none of these things were true. The other problem was that, despite discussing these factors at length, I remained profoundly ill. I would eat in the hospital or at a residential treatment centre, where I was sent when my condition deteriorated, but then I would return to my old ways upon discharge. I was 29 years old, and despite two advanced degrees, I had to come to terms with the fact that I didn't have the first clue as to how to feed myself appropriately. My once-vibrant life had narrowed to the number on the scale and my next meal. Nothing else mattered, and no one could figure out why.

"It wasn't until nearly a decade after I was diagnosed that a therapist told me that, not only was my eating disorder no one's fault, the personality traits that were driving the anorexia (perfectionism, attention to detail, a drive to achieve) could actually be beneficial. I learned about some of the biology that explained why I was

so vulnerable to anorexia, and why not eating actually made me feel less anxious and less depressed. Instead of demonising my parents as the cause of the anorexia, we needed to utilise them as supports to help me get better. The shift was profound. What we created was a specialised anorexia treatment programme with a clientele of one: me. Food was described as medicine, and I was expected to eat everything I was served. I would rather have jumped out of a plane without a parachute, and if I had known someone with a pilot's licence, I might have. Meal by meal, snack by snack, however, the eating disorder began to loosen its grasp.

"Now, nearly six years later, I don't describe myself as 'fully recovered'. I still follow a food plan that helps me decide how much I need to eat. I have entered into a fragile détente with my weight, grudgingly accepting that I am mentally and physically healthier in my current state even if I feel like evidence of a new species of land whale most of the time. Nor am I free of relapse. I have had two major relapses in the past few years, one of them rather recently. My organ systems are no longer nearly as forgiving as they were when my disease started. My bones are irreversibly damaged, and it takes little to throw my heart into complete chaos. Despite all of this, I have managed to create a life worth living and that, in and of itself, is a feat for someone who was repeatedly written off as uncooperative and untreatable.

"In my years of being involved with the larger eating disorder community, I have seen a profound shift in the way we think about eating disorders. Although far too many people are still told that their disorder is 'about control' or that there's nothing anyone can do until a person chooses to get well, many parents and sufferers are learning about the complex web of biological and environmental ingredients that come together to create an eating disorder. I recently spent a week in Ohio observing a treatment programme that brings this all together – the NEW FED TR programme that I wrote about for Mosaic. It was a sea-change compared to what I experienced so many years ago.

"Other adults with anorexia like me need programmes like NEW FED TR. We also need other options, too, like meal coaches and halfway houses and tailored inpatient and outpatient programmes. The people I've met both online and off have amazing potential, fuelled by the very same traits that also fuel their disorders. Learning to use those traits 'for good instead of evil', as my therapist likes to say, is one of the major tasks of recovery.

"I may never feel at ease with food or learn to love my body, but my recovery doesn't have to be perfect to be wonderful."

29 March 2016

⇨ The above information is reprinted with kind permission from Carrie Arnold and Mosaic. Please visit mosaicscience.com for further information.

# Anorexia nervosa – treatment

The treatment for anorexia nervosa usually involves a combination of psychological therapy and supervised weight gain.

It's important for a person with anorexia to start treatment as early as possible to reduce the risk of serious complications of anorexia, particularly if they've already lost a lot of weight.

## The treatment plan

GPs are often closely involved in ongoing treatment, although other healthcare professionals are usually involved, including:

⇨ specialist counsellors

⇨ psychiatrists

⇨ psychologists

⇨ specialist nurses

⇨ dietitians

⇨ paediatricians in cases affecting children and teenagers.

Before treatment starts, members of this multidisciplinary care team will carry out a detailed physical, psychological and social needs assessment, and will develop a care plan.

Most people with anorexia are treated as an outpatient, which means they visit hospitals, specialist centres or individual members of their care team for appointments, but return home in between.

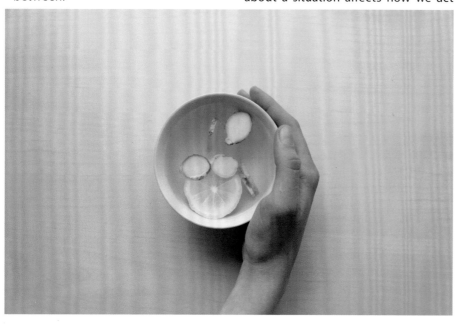

In more severe cases, a person may need to stay in hospital or a specialist centre for longer periods during the day (day patient), or they may need to be admitted as an inpatient.

## Psychological treatment

A number of different psychological treatments can be used to treat anorexia. Depending on the severity of the condition, treatment will last for at least six to 12 months or more.

## Cognitive analytic therapy (CAT)

Cognitive analytic therapy (CAT) is based on the theory that mental health conditions such as anorexia are caused by unhealthy patterns of behaviour and thinking developed in the past, usually during childhood.

CAT involves a three-stage process:

⇨ reformulation – looking at past events that may explain why the unhealthy patterns developed

⇨ recognition – helping people see how these patterns are contributing towards the anorexia

⇨ revision – identifying changes that can break these unhealthy patterns.

## Cognitive behavioural therapy (CBT)

Cognitive behavioural therapy (CBT) is based on the theory that how we think about a situation affects how we act

and, in turn, our actions can affect how we think and feel.

In terms of anorexia, the therapist will attempt to show how the condition is often associated with unhealthy and unrealistic thoughts and beliefs about food and diet.

For example, these could be:

"Putting on weight is the single worst thing that can happen in my life."

"Everyone I know secretly thinks I'm fat."

"If I finish the whole meal, people I'm eating with will think I'm greedy and worthless."

The therapist will encourage the adoption of healthier, more realistic ways of thinking that should lead to more positive behaviour.

## Interpersonal therapy (IPT)

Interpersonal therapy (IPT) is based on the theory that relationships with other people and the outside world in general have a powerful effect on mental health.

Anorexia may be associated with feelings of low self-esteem, anxiety and self-doubt caused by problems interacting with people.

During IPT, the therapist will explore negative issues associated with your interpersonal relationships and how these issues can be resolved.

## Focal psychodynamic therapy (FPT)

Focal psychodynamic therapy (FPT) is based on the theory that mental health conditions may be associated with unresolved conflicts that occurred in the past, usually during childhood.

The therapy encourages people with anorexia to think about how early childhood experiences may have affected them. The aim is to find more successful ways of coping with stressful situations and negative thoughts and emotions.

## Family interventions

Anorexia doesn't just impact on one individual – it can have a big impact on the whole family. Family intervention

is an important part of treatment for young people with anorexia.

Family intervention should focus on the eating disorder, and involves the family discussing how anorexia has affected them. It can also help the family understand the condition and how they can help.

## Gaining weight safely

The care plan will include advice about how to increase the amount eaten so weight is gained safely.

Physical health – as well as weight – is monitored closely. The height of children and young people will also be regularly checked to make sure they're developing as expected.

To begin with, the person will be given small amounts of food to eat, with the amount gradually increasing as their body gets used to dealing with normal amounts.

The eventual aim is to have a regular eating pattern, with three meals a day, possibly with vitamin and mineral supplements.

An outpatient target is an average gain of 0.5kg (1.1lbs) a week. In a specialist unit, the aim will usually be to gain an average of around 0.5–1kg (1.1–2.2lbs) a week.

## Compulsory treatment

Occasionally, someone with anorexia may refuse treatment even though they're severely ill and their life is at risk.

In these cases, as a last resort doctors may decide to admit the person to hospital for compulsory treatment under the Mental Health Act. This is sometimes known as sectioning or being sectioned.

## Treating additional problems

As well as the main treatments mentioned above, other health problems caused by anorexia will also need to be treated.

If you make yourself vomit regularly, you'll be given dental hygiene advice to help prevent stomach acid damaging the enamel on your teeth.

For example, you may be advised not to brush your teeth soon after vomiting to avoid further abrasion to tooth enamel, and to rinse out your mouth with water instead.

Avoiding acidic foods and mouth washes may be recommended. You'll also be advised to visit a dentist regularly so they can check for any problems.

If you've been taking laxatives or diuretics in an attempt to lose weight, you'll be advised to reduce them gradually so your body can adjust. Stopping them suddenly can cause problems such as nausea and constipation.

## Medication

Medication alone isn't usually effective in treating anorexia. It's often only used in combination with the measures mentioned above to treat associated psychological problems, such as obsessive compulsive disorder (OCD) or depression.

Two of the main types of medication used to treat people with anorexia are:

⇨ selective serotonin reuptake inhibitors (SSRIs) – a type of antidepressant medication that can help people with co-existing psychological problems such as depression and anxiety

⇨ olanzapine – a medication that can help reduce feelings of anxiety related to issues such as weight and diet in people who haven't responded to other treatments

SSRIs tend to be avoided until a person with anorexia has started to gain weight because the risk of more serious side effects is increased in people who are severely underweight. The drugs are only used cautiously in young people under the age of 18.

## Help and support

If you have an eating disorder or know someone who does, you may find it useful to contact a support group such as Beat for information and advice.

Beat provides:

⇨ a confidential adult helpline on 0808 801 0677 – they also have a designated youth helpline on 0808 801 0711 (both helplines are open every day of the year from 4pm to 10pm)

⇨ live chat and online support groups, where you can talk to others in a similar situation

⇨ a national network of volunteer support groups

You can also use the Beat HelpFinder directory to find eating disorder support services in your local area.

*26 January 2016*

⇨ The above information is reprinted with kind permission from NHS Choices. Please visit www.nhs.uk for further information.

*© NHS Choices 2017*

# A grown-up approach to treating anorexia

*Adults with anorexia often have distinctive traits that lock them into a destructive relationship with food. Carrie Arnold discovers how those same traits could help them escape it.*

Heather Purdin had run out of options. Aged 33, she had been suffering from anorexia nervosa for more than two decades and her weight had plummeted to that of a small child, an all-time low for her. Her case worker, out of frustration and desperation, suggested hospice care as a way to spend her remaining days in relative comfort. But for the first time in years, Heather was sure of one thing: she desperately wanted to live.

Treating anorexia, which is characterised by self-starvation and an inability to maintain an adequate body weight, seems absurdly simple on the surface: just eat and gain weight. It's something Heather and the millions of others afflicted by eating disorders have heard countless times. The problem is that it's never that simple. Heather has long since lost track of the number of times she has been admitted to hospital for low body weight, electrolyte imbalances caused by starvation or self-induced vomiting, or thoughts of suicide. In hospital she gains weight, but as soon as she is discharged she promptly returns to her old ways and loses what little weight she has gained. And so for more than 20 years, she has remained hopelessly, incurably, stuck.

Up to one in five people with chronic anorexia may die as a result of their illness, either due to the direct effects of starvation and malnutrition or due to suicide, making it the deadliest of all psychiatric disorders. Although scientists have made tremendous progress in decoding the underlying biology of eating disorders and in finding ways to intervene in cases of teenage anorexia before the disorder becomes chronic, this hasn't translated into effective treatments for adults like Heather.

A chance posting on Facebook last autumn, however, brought Heather the first breath of hope she had felt in years. In Ohio, there was an experimental five-day intensive programme to help adults with anorexia. What made this one different was that it used the latest neurobiology research to mould its goals as well as how its treatment was delivered. And since research confirms that most patients struggle to make changes to their entrenched behaviours on their own, patients also had to invite up to four support people to join them on the residential programme. Heather asked her father and her sister, and began raising the funds to fly them all to Ohio.

"I need this to work," she said. "I have nothing else to try."

Despite its reputation as a quintessentially modern disorder, anorexia is nothing new. Historians believe that many of the 'fasting saints' of the Middle Ages had anorexia. The first medical report of the illness appeared in 1689, written by London physician Richard Morton, who described it as "a Nervous Consumption" caused by "Sadness and anxious Cares".

Even as recently as the 1970s, anorexia remained something of a clinical oddity – a disease that doctors rarely saw, let alone had a clue how to treat. When psychologist Laura Hill saw her first anorexia patient at a university counselling centre back in 1979, she had never even heard of the disorder: "Her father was in the science department there and I had to ask him what anorexia was," recalls Hill. "He told me she was unable to gain weight, afraid of food."

Rates of anorexia had been steadily climbing since the 1950s, but it wasn't until the death of singer Karen Carpenter in 1983 that the disorder became a household word. She died from heart failure due to anorexia nervosa, and all of a sudden newspaper stories and after-school TV specials began to feature teenage girls "dying to be thin". Besides highlighting the spectacle of a healthy, attractive young girl's determination to starve herself, the storylines usually focused on the family dysfunction that psychologists believed lay at the heart of the disorder. Parents were told not to be the food police, that anorexia was a misguided search for control. Only when they let their child be fully in control of their own life would the anorexia resolve.

Psychiatrist Walter Kaye wasn't convinced. Despite not having done research into eating disorders before, he had been asked to help finish an anorexia study for the US National Institutes of Health in the early 1980s. While talking with the participants, he noticed something unusual.

"I was just kind of struck by how homogenous the symptoms were," he says. Because the patients seemed so similar in terms of symptoms and temperament, he believed there had to be something in their biology that was causing anorexia – and he dedicated himself to finding out what it was.

In the early 1980s, anorexia had been seen by the medical community as a deliberate decision by a petulant teenage girl: she was selfish, vain, wilful. Since she had chosen to become ill, she simply needed to choose to get better. She needed to become a fully formed individual, to separate from her family and rebel against the cultural ideal of thinness at all costs.

Scientific research by Kaye and others, however, exploded every aspect of this stereotype (not least that anorexia only affects girls) and completely changed how we think about the condition. Psychologists like Laura Hill had to rethink their whole approach: "Many times, I want to call up all my old patients and apologise for getting so much backwards," she says.

Hill began to keep a file full of notes about what she thought was causing anorexia, what her patients believed, what seemed to work and what didn't. After a few years, she entered a PhD programme to better help her patients. But even with several research articles to her name and, ultimately, decades working at the forefront of treating and researching eating disorders, she realised that the treatment advances weren't reaching adults with anorexia. She wasn't the only one. Across the field, psychologists, psychiatrists and dietitians have noted that treatment outcomes for adults with anorexia remain abysmally low. Less than half recover fully, another third show some improvement, but the rest remain chronically ill.

"They go for many years, and they've relapsed over and over again, and they have the highest risk of dying," says Kaye. "I think all of us are feeling that this is a serious, often deadly disorder for these people, and we don't have good approaches, and we don't understand enough about the causes."

For adolescents with anorexia, a ground-breaking treatment developed at the Maudsley Hospital in London in the 1980s called family-based treatment (FBT) has significantly improved short-term recovery outcomes. It puts parents temporarily in charge of making food and exercise decisions for their child and places a priority on normalising weight and eating habits. In a randomised clinical trial published in 2010, around half of teens treated with FBT met criteria for full recovery after a year, compared to 23 per cent of teens receiving standard treatment.

Nothing has been remotely that successful for adults with anorexia, and there's no easy explanation as to why. One reason may be that adults have simply been sicker for longer, says Angela Guarda, Director of the Eating Disorders Program at Johns Hopkins University: "The longer you have anorexia, the more anorexia creates physiological changes in the body and the brain that then create a self-sustaining cycle. You do it today because you did it yesterday, no longer because you decided to go on the Atkins diet when you were 15 or because your coach said something to you or you broke up with a boyfriend and you decided to lose weight. It's no longer about that."

As well, many people with anorexia don't grasp that they are, in fact, sick. While parents generally sign their children into treatment, that power vanishes when the child turns 18. Adult patients can also stop treatment if it gets too difficult – and it often does, because challenging the behaviours associated with eating disorders can create tidal waves of anxiety. A long-term, chronic eating disorder often ends up alienating friends and family, the very people who tend to push their ill loved one into treatment and support them through the recovery process.

Clinicians, like their patients, are desperate for something better, some way not only to help adults with anorexia normalise their eating and gain weight, but also

to help them stay well. "In anorexia, you get their weight up and they go home straight from inpatient [where] they're fed from a tray, and they're expected to know how to eat in a restaurant, eat in a cafeteria, eat in social settings, when they haven't been eating with anyone for a decade," Guarda says.

On a warm spring weekend in 2006, Laura Hill stopped in the middle of mowing her lawn. She had spent the morning reading one of Walter Kaye's articles on the neurobiology of anorexia, and was familiar with how Kaye and his colleague Stephanie Knatz were beginning to use neurobiology in designing new treatments for adolescents. It occurred to Hill that she could do something similar for her adult patients.

She dashed inside to grab a pad of paper and a pencil, where she scribbled a few notes before returning to her lawn. Several passes later, she had another insight and again stopped mowing to add to her notes. This went on all afternoon. It took until dusk to finish the mowing, but by then, as well as a neatly cut lawn, Hill also had the outline of a new type of adult anorexia treatment that would harness the strengths of people with the disorder and try to compensate for their weaknesses.

She continued to work on the outline, asking her patients at the Center for Balanced Living in Ohio for input on what they found helpful. A few years later, she teamed up with Kaye and Knatz, who further refined the idea based on their experiences at the University of California, San Diego. There, they had had remarkable success with a five-day intensive FBT programme for adolescents. Rather than seeing someone once a week, which might not be enough to be effective, or taking them away from their family and putting them in an artificial environment for a residential programme, they had insisted that the family come and stay too. Encouragingly, some young adults – living at home or supported by their parents – had also taken part, suggesting that this format could work with an older crowd as well.

"As opposed to having people step in for an hour and talk about what happened over the week, we're actually seeing what happens live, in vivo. That gives us the possibility to intervene in vivo, as opposed to coaching people on what

they should do 'when circumstances come up'," says Knatz.

In 2013, Hill, Knatz and Kaye applied for a grant from the US National Eating Disorders Association to fund a pilot study of what they called Neurobiologically Enhanced With Family/Friends Eating Disorder Trait Response (NEW FED TR). Every aspect of the programme was based on what researchers understood about what happens in the brain of someone with anorexia, the goal being not just to improve treatment but also to reduce blame and guilt among sufferers and families. To that end, NEW FED TR would involve care givers and loved ones as an integral part of treatment, creating a team that could work to fight the eating disorder together. Responsibility for recovery would remain firmly in each client's hands, but some aspects of recovery that tend to be sticking points for adults with anorexia could be outsourced to their support people as needed.

On an unusually mild Monday morning in December 2015, Heather Purdin was fiddling with the ponytail securing her dark brown hair, just as she always does when she's nervous. It was a short drive from the hotel, across the freeway interchange to the back of a wooded business park. Her body mass index (BMI) was very low now – all muscle and softness stripped from her body, leaving only sinew and bone. A baggy shirt and scarf couldn't conceal how ill she was. But she was not on her way to a hospital or a hospice. Flanked by her father, sister and best friend, she entered the Center for Balanced Living to take her place on the successfully funded pilot of the NEW FED TR programme. And despite all her fears, a giant grin lit up her face.

It looks like any other kitchen. Long, grey countertops line one wall and an island; there's a large stove, a sink and a fridge. Beau Barley, a tall, thin 20-year-old with bleached blond hair and a two-day-old beard, is cooking an omelette for breakfast while his parents prepare their own meals. It could be breakfast at any home in America, except that Beau is at the Center for Balanced Living, on his second day of the NEW FED TR programme.

"Okay, clients, check in with your supports to make sure you've got enough to eat," calls the programme's dietitian, Sonja

Stotz. She listens in as Beau shows his meal of eggs, toast, butter, milk and fruit to his parents.

Like around half of those with anorexia, Beau suffered from obsessive–compulsive disorder (OCD) as a child, having to turn off lights in a certain way and avoid all the cracks on the sidewalk. Every time he heard a siren, he had to call his mum because he thought she had been in an accident because he didn't do one of his rituals right.

Always sporty, his anorexia started with a simple desire to be a better runner on his high school cross-country team. He ramped up his mileage, running longer and longer each day and eventually training year-round. The sport he loved became a compulsion. But overtraining eventually took a toll and he was sidelined by a severe stress fracture. His only thought as his leg was being X-rayed in the hospital was that he needed to cut back on his food if he wanted to stay in shape for next season. As his mother pushed him out of the emergency room in a wheelchair, she asked him what he wanted for dinner. "A salad," he replied.

From there, Beau became more and more obsessed with eating 'healthy' and returning to running. At first, his weight was stable. But as his running obsession returned, his metabolism kicked in. Always somewhat slender, his weight plummeted. In the summer before he started university, he went through his first formal treatment programme at the Center for Balanced Living, attending group therapy during the day, eating his meals at the centre and returning home every night. Things started to look up, but Beau relapsed during his first year at university. Over the past summer and autumn, he has tried to make progress against his eating disorder, but the exercise compulsion is cemented in place. When his mother called the centre to see if he could return, they recommended NEW FED TR. Beau eagerly signed up and now here he is, showing his parents what he has cooked for himself this morning.

"Are those all your exchanges?" his mother asks. NEW FED TR uses a meal plan that assigns each individual a certain number of choices or 'exchanges' from each food group for every meal and snack.

He indicates that it is, telling her how the food on his plate adds up to his prescribed meal. Satisfied with his choices, Stotz moves on to assist one of the three other families in the kitchen. Beau's family sit down at the table and, as breakfast begins, Hill and Stotz suggest fun games to play as a distraction, to decrease the anxiety all of the clients feel around eating. The less anxiety they feel, the more likely they are to successfully complete the meal, which serves as their medication.

Stotz points out that her job is selling her patients on the idea that they need to eat more and exercise less, the very opposite of what most dietitians do. "I should go into sales," she laughs.

In the morning sessions, Hill gives the clients and their families a crash course on eating disorder neurobiology. Eating disorders typically begin in adolescence, and anorexia is no different. Although the exact circumstances that trigger the onset of anorexia aren't clear, nearly all cases begin when a person fails to meet their energy needs, placing them in a state of what researchers call negative energy balance – burning more calories than they eat. For some, a weight-loss diet precipitates the eating disorder; for others, it's increased sports training, a growth spurt, an illness, decreased appetite from stress, even new braces.

For most people, being in a negative energy balance is profoundly uncomfortable. That's why dieting often makes people impulsive and cranky, 'hangry' even. But those with a predisposition for anorexia have a completely different experience. Starvation makes them feel better.

Kaye's work with women who have recovered from anorexia nervosa found unusually high levels of the neurotransmitter serotonin in the cerebrospinal fluid that bathes the brain, and he believes these levels were likely also present before the onset of anorexia. Although low serotonin levels are linked to depression, high serotonin levels aren't good either, as they create a state of chronic anxiety and irritability. As many as three-quarters of those with anorexia had suffered from an anxiety disorder before their eating disorder began, most commonly social anxiety and OCD. It is this anxiety that Kaye believes makes some people much more vulnerable to anorexia.

The body synthesises serotonin from the amino acid tryptophan, which we get from our diet. Eat less food and you get less tryptophan and hence less serotonin. For people predisposed to anorexia, therefore, starvation reduces the anxiety and irritability associated with their high serotonin levels. Mission accomplished, or so it seems. The problem is that the brain fights back, increasing the number of receptors for serotonin to wring every last drop out of the neurotransmitter that is there. This increased sensitivity means that the old negative feelings return, which drives the person to cut back even more on what they're eating. Any attempts to return to normal eating patterns wind up flooding the hypersensitive brain with a surge of serotonin, creating panic, rage and emotional instability. Anorexia has, in effect, locked itself into place.

Heather Purdin and her team see this first-hand as Hill asks the different groups of clients and supports to use yarn, taken from Hill's massive collection of weaving supplies, to wind the client's hands into place. Heather's team rapidly pin her hands and arms in front of her face. This, Hill says, is the anorexia in action. Heather is now as stuck physically as she is mentally. Getting her functioning again means weaving her supports into her mental 'loom'. Here is where the team struggle, especially when Hill asks Heather what she is going to do differently. In sheer frustration, she slams her knotted hands onto the table in front of her.

"It's not working," she wails. "I can't change."

The tears start and it doesn't seem they will ever stop. It is, however, her lightbulb moment.

"I realised I wasn't completely crazy," Heather says later. "It was a huge relief. It is real and I'm not making it up and I'm not a complete loser."

Recovering from anorexia, Hill says, is like learning to navigate around landmines. They can be deadly, and they can derail recovery. One of the biggest struggles for people with anorexia is making decisions: a first-year university student on the programme, who asked not to be named, admits that she can stand in front of the fridge for hours trying to decide what to have for lunch. Frustrated, she often shuts the door without eating anything.

Hill rounds everyone up and asks them

to toss their treatment binders into the centre of the room. One by one, the clients are asked to close their eyes and walk across the room without bumping into anything. Not surprisingly, no one can do it. But when they ask a family member to guide them, they get safely to the other side. In real life, this could mean the university student asking one of her parents to pack her lunch for her if she becomes too anxious to make a healthy decision.

"People with eating disorders have many amazing qualities, and like anything it has both positives and negatives," says Hill. The goal of the programme is to make these traits work for an individual as much as possible, and to enlist loved ones to fill in for the parts of the brain that might not be working properly.

The exact details of this are hammered out by each family throughout the week in the Recovery Support Agreement. Skipping meals or snacks or not gaining weight as appropriate could result in consequences that are agreed in advance, like leaving university or eating more meals with supports.

"It's helpful for people with anorexia because they like rules, they like structure, they don't like the unknown, so they have a pretty good idea of what's going to happen if they're not able to eat and gain weight. And our data is suggesting that may be a useful approach," says Kaye.

A 2003 study identified five personality traits that increased the risk of developing an eating disorder: perfectionism, inflexibility, having to follow the rules, excessive doubt and caution, and a drive for order and symmetry. Other studies have found links between anxiety, perfectionism and anorexia. Adults with anorexia get stuck on details and have trouble zooming out to see the big picture, which can make it difficult to make decisions. As well, they have difficulty mentally switching from one task to the next.

For too long, says Hill, eating disorder professionals have been focusing on these traits as weaknesses when that's not true. To succeed at scientific research, for instance, obsessionality and attention to detail is almost a must. Since people with anorexia use rules and routines to 'succeed' at their eating disorder, they can also learn to use them to succeed at recovery. It sounds like a small shift, but

for anorexia sufferers like Heather and Beau, it makes all the difference in the world.

"Make your quirks work," Heather quips with a smile.

"Ew, don't eat that," says the mother of the first-year university student. She isn't providing feedback at mealtime now but playing the role of the insula, a region of the brain that is sensitive to disgust. Other participants role-play other regions in a re-enactment of how the brain makes decisions around food.

In healthy individuals, determining what and how much to eat is controlled by a variety of factors, including what's available, how much it's liked and how hungry the person is. Not so in anorexia. Kaye's work using functional magnetic resonance imaging (fMRI) of the brain has teased out other important details. Unlike most people, whose brains respond strongly to rewarding things such as sweets, people with anorexia are generally far more sensitive to punishment (the removal of something pleasant) than reward.

Another study found that the brains of women who had recovered from anorexia responded significantly less to sugar water than healthy controls, and they found sweets less rewarding when hungry. Kaye says these results may indicate how they are able to continue starving even while food is plentiful, since people with anorexia find food less rewarding and thus have less motivation to eat. Tests also showed a preoccupation with future harm at the expense of what might be needed in the present moment.

"One reason that people with anorexia are able to starve themselves is that when they get hungry, the parts of the brain that should be driving reward and motivation just aren't getting activated," he says.

So when it's time to role-play the 'anorexia brain' considering whether or not to take a bite of banana, those people playing brain regions responsible for reward (the feeling of 'yum!' when you eat a piece of chocolate cake) are quiet, while the brain areas responsible for worry kick into overdrive. The result is that no one in the room can hear the small, quiet part of the brain telling the person with anorexia it is okay to eat the banana.

Hill plays an audio recording of one of her

former patients re-enacting the anorexic thoughts that tormented her while she ate – it is an endless stream of "I can't eat this. I'm going to get fat. I'm ugly. I'm disgusting. I'm weak. I hate myself. I can't do this. I'm so pathetic, just pathetic, a weak pig." It goes on for more than ten minutes.

Parents, many of whom had walked into the programme frustrated and angry at their child's seeming refusal to eat, hear the recording and the sheer amount of 'noise' that their children endure and their anger dissipates.

"I get it now," Beau's mum says, dabbing at her eyes with a tissue. "I get it."

Heather's week at the NEW FED TR programme has been life-altering: "For the first time, someone got what I had been saying all along, that I had a biologically based brain disorder," she says. "They worked with me instead of against me."

By December 2015, nearly 25 families had participated in NEW FED TR, and more pilot groups are in the works. Feedback, Hill says, has been uniformly positive, even from those with anorexia – pretty rare for a treatment programme that requires a person to face their deepest fears six times a day, eating three meals and three snacks. It's too soon to say whether the programme has been effective in helping adult anorexia sufferers move towards recovery, but for Heather it marks the first time she has actually believed in her own ability to get better.

For the first time in 20 years, she says simply, "I have hope." And with that, she heads to Trader Joe's to buy ingredients for a Christmas feast she is hosting for friends and family. It would have been unimaginable last year, but now she hopes it will become a tradition that will continue for a very long time.

*29 March 2016*

⇨  The above information is reprinted with kind permission from Carrie Arnold and Mosaic. Please visit www.mosaicscience.com for further information.

# Deep brain stimulation can help women with anorexia gain weight, study finds

*By Cristina Silva*

Deep brain stimulation could help health officials treat severe anorexia nervosa and reduce depression and anxiety, a new study released this week found. Deep brain stimulation involves implanting electrodes deep in the brain and could help drive weight gain, BBC News reported Friday.

**"Eating disorders such as anorexia nervosa, bulimia nervosa and binge-eating disorder tend to be more common in women than men. They often develop during adolescence or early adulthood"**

The study published in *The Lancet Psychiatry* journal involved 16 women with severe anorexia between the ages of 21 and 57. The participants all had anorexia for an average of nearly two decades and tried other treatment without success. Some of the women faced early death because of their anorexia.

The study saw electrodes placed in specific areas of their brains associated with anorexia. After a few months, some of the women said their depression and anxiety had lessened. After a year, many of the women had put on weight. In all, the participants' body mass index soared from 13.8 to 17.3. Brain scans also showed changes in the areas linked to anorexia.

"There are currently no effective treatments for people with long-standing anorexia nervosa – people who are often the sickest and most vulnerable of dying from the condition," Dr Nir Lipsman, a neurosurgeon at the Sunnybrook Health Sciences Centre, told the BBC. "Our work, which builds on earlier trials, is one of the first brain-based strategies that has been shown to help with chronic anorexia. And my hope is that through this research we are also validating the idea that anorexia is a brain-based illness, not a personality or lifestyle choice."

Researchers, however, warned larger studies would also need to show-deep brain stimulation works before the therapy becomes a go-to treatment plan for health officials. There were also problems with the study. One patient had a seizure and two people wanted their electrodes be removed during the trial.

**"Deep brain stimulation could help health officials treat treat severe anorexia nervosa and reduce depression and anxiety, a new study released this week found. Deep brain stimulation involves implanting electrodes deep in the brain and could help drive weight gain"**

"Further work to establish efficacy, safety and long-term outcomes in a larger cohort is needed," Dr Carrie McAdams, of the University of Texas Southwestern, wrote of the study.

Eating disorders such as anorexia nervosa, bulimia nervosa and binge-eating disorder tend to be more common in women than men. They often develop during adolescence or early adulthood.

Deep brain stimulation is currently used to treat Parkinson's disease symptoms.

*25 February 2017*

⇨ The above information is reprinted with kind permission from the *International Business Times*. Please visit www.ibtimes.com for further information.

# Best treatments for binge-eating disorder revealed in new review

*"A person who binge eats uses food as a means of coping with, or silencing, negative emotions such as anxiety or depression."*

*By Natasha Hinde*

People with binge-eating disorder can be best helped with talk therapy or medication, according to a review of studies on the subject.

Binge eating can be defined as "consuming large amounts of food in a short period of time". Often, a person will eat until they become uncomfortably full.

"A person who binge eats uses food as a means of coping with, or silencing, negative emotions such as anxiety or depression," a spokesperson for eating disorders charity Beat told The Huffington Post UK.

An independent review of previous studies on the eating disorder concluded that cognitive behavioural therapy (CBT) could help reduce binge-eating.

Similarly, a class of drugs known as second-generation antidepressants, as well as the amphetamine called lisdexamfetamine (or Vyvanse) helped ease symptoms among sufferers.

The review has been welcomed by Beat who said there "hasn't been enough research carried out on binge-eating disorder".

"Reviews such as this are crucial in informing clinical guidance such as the NICE guidelines – due in 2017 – and improving clinical practice," said a spokesperson.

Bingeing can be a very secretive and guilt-ridden experience. Sufferers will uncontrollably eat, hiding away so that others cannot see them.

The condition tends to first develop in young adults, although many people do not seek help until they are in their 30s or 40s.

It is estimated that the disorder affects 350,000 people in the UK.

People with binge-eating disorder can spend "abnormal" amounts of money on food. They will then eat in secret, so that the amount of food being consumed is not observed.

"Because of the amount of food eaten, many people with binge eating disorder can become obese," said Beat's spokesperson. "This can lead to problems with blood pressure, heart disease and a general lack of fitness."

The disorder can result in health issues including stomach pain, irregular periods in females, poor or spotty skin, constipation and sleeping difficulties.

Researchers from the University of North Carolina at Chapel Hill analysed data from nine studies of psychological treatments and 25 studies of medications in patients with binge-eating disorder.

They found that CBT helped people to identify thoughts associated with binge-eating and helped them to change their behaviours.

Meanwhile the medications reduced obsessions and compulsions related to the disorder, including decreasing a person's impulse to eat.

Examples of second-generation antidepressants include citalopram (Celexa), escitalopram (Lexapro), fluoxetine (Prozac), paroxetine (Paxil) and sertraline (Zoloft).

The review couldn't help researchers determine whether one second-generation antidepressant was better than others. Similarly, they couldn't say that any of the treatment types were fundamentally better than others.

"There have been no head-to-head (comparisons) and that's really essential," said lead author Kimberly Brownley.

The review shows that treatments are available and people don't have to suffer through the disorder alone, she added.

> **"Binge eating can be defined as 'consuming large amounts of food in a short period of time'"**

For those who might be reading this and feeling concerned about their own attitudes towards eating, the next best step is to seek help and support.

"For yourself, do try to tell someone you trust," advised a Beat spokesperson. "They are likely to be more understanding than you realise, and having someone 'on your side' will make it so much easier to make the changes you will need to overcome your difficulties."

For people who are worried about a family member or friend, they added: "Don't be afraid to talk to them and offer support. The chances are they are desperately hoping someone will notice and reach out to them.

"Try to understand and ask about what is worrying them, rather than blame and shame them – they already feel dreadful, and that doesn't help. Talking about their feelings, rather than the food is a good starting point."

*29 June 2016*

⇨ The above information is reprinted with kind permission from The Huffington Post UK. Please visit www.huffingtonpost.co.uk for further information.

# Bulimia treatment

## Bulimia nervosa is getting rid of food by purging, taking laxatives and even excessive exercise.

### Bulimia Nervosa: is this you?

#### Emotions and behaviour

⇨ You feel out of control of food; you are desperate to control your weight but eat compulsively at times.

⇨ Bulimia feels like an addiction. Eating rules your life.

⇨ You are fearful of weight gain and feel very bad about your body and shape. You act as if you were confident but your self-esteem is low.

⇨ You may promise to stop your bulimia, but it somehow doesn't happen and you are ashamed in case people discover what is going on.

⇨ Food feels like a friend and a foe, wish you could just take it or leave it.

⇨ You have mood swings, often for no reason; you feel depressed, alone and low.

⇨ You have started purging as a desperate way to control your weight, but it isn't working well and your weight may start increasing.

#### Physical outcomes

The right help for bulimia will help to heal the side effects, which can include surface problems, with teeth and salivation glands; deeper problems affecting fertility and the digestive system; cardiac and brain effects.

#### Getting help

Bulimia treatment and help begins here. It is better to get help sooner rather than later, Even after many years, recovery is possible with the right support from us.

#### Recovery aims

Bulimia treatment means a new relationship with food and self-control with food and weight. Help for bulimia also means emotional strengthening, raising self worth and finding better ways of feeling in control without needing to purge. We start with a full assessment, to help build a personalised treatment plan that is right for you.

### Bulimia treatment takes time and will focus on

⇨ Gaining insight about bulimia and discovering what led to you developing it in the first place.

⇨ Managing the mixed feelings about letting it go and building motivation to change.

⇨ Nutritional guidance, to end compulsive eating and manage overeating without the need to purge. You will not gain weight.

⇨ Emotional strengthening, to manage feelings like stress and unhappiness without turning to food or purging.

⇨ Managing bulimic thoughts and obsessions with food.

⇨ Self worth and body image healing.

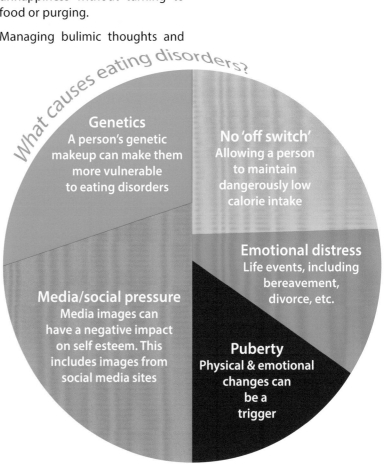

*Source: Based on information from the Royal College of Psychiatrists (2014) Anorexia and Bulimia, Available at: http://www.rcpsych.ac.uk/healthadvice/problemsdisorders/anorexiaandbulimia.aspx As reproduced by b-eat in their report The costs of eating disorders, February 2015.*

# Supporting someone with an eating disorder

*If your friend or relative has an eating disorder, such as anorexia, bulimia or binge eating disorder, you will probably want to do everything you can to help them recover.*

You're already doing a great job by finding out more about eating disorders and how to try and support them – it shows you care and helps you understand how they might be feeling.

Getting professional help from a doctor, practice nurse, or a school or college nurse will give your friend or relative the best chance of getting better. But this can be one of the most difficult steps for someone suffering from an eating disorder, so try to encourage them to seek help or offer to go along with them.

You can support them in other ways, too:

⇨ Keep trying to include them – they may not want to go out or join in with activities, but despite this, keep trying to talk to them and ask them along, just like before. Even if they don't join in, they will still like to be asked. It will make them feel valued as a person.

⇨ Try to build up their self-esteem, perhaps by telling them what a great person they are and how much you appreciate having them in your life.

⇨ Give your time and listen to them, and try not to give advice or criticise. This can be tough when you don't agree with what they say about themselves and what they eat. Remember, you don't have to know all the answers. Just making sure they know you're there for them is what's important. This is especially true when it feels like your friend or relative is rejecting your friendship, help and support.

## How are eating disorders treated?

Treatment for eating disorders varies around the country. Different types of help may be offered depending on where you live.

Treatment looks to deal with the emotional issues as well as the physical, but this must be done slowly so your friend or relative is able to cope with the changes.

Treatment will involve your friend or relative talking to someone about the emotional difficulties that have led to their eating disorder. It will also explore their physical problems, general health and eating patterns. Help with eating and putting on weight alone is usually not enough.

The earlier your friend or relative starts the treatment programme and the more they engage with it, the better their chances of making a good recovery.

## Will they have to go into hospital?

Most people with eating disorders will not have to stay in hospital. They are seen as outpatients, which means they visit the hospital, for example, one day a week.

Some people who have a more advanced or serious eating disorder might need to visit the hospital more often, or be admitted to hospital for more intensive support and treatment (known as inpatient care).

## Should I visit them in hospital?

This depends on what your friend or relative wants, how you feel and what the treatment centre allows. Let them know you're thinking of them and would like to visit them. If this is not possible, you can always write to them or call to let them know you're still there to support them.

## Can people be forced to get help for eating disorders?

If your friend or relative has lost an extreme amount of weight, they may be in danger of starving themselves and developing serious complications. They may not be able to think clearly because of the lack of food and may have to be forced into life-saving treatment.

In these circumstances, their doctor may decide to admit them to hospital for specialist treatment. This can only be done after the doctor has consulted with colleagues and they all agree with the doctor's decision. This is called being sectioned and it is done under the rules of the Mental Health Act.

## Will they be cured when they come home?

Your friend or relative will still need your support. Most people with an eating disorder do recover and learn to use more positive ways of coping.

But recovery from an eating disorder can be very difficult and can take a long time. Your friend or relative may even relapse into old behaviours, or have periods of living with their illness again during their recovery.

Part of them may want to get better, while the other part might be very scared about giving up the eating disorder. They might think, "I want to get better, but just don't want to gain weight."

They will probably have good days and bad days. During times of stress, the eating difficulties may be more likely to return. Changing the way people with eating disorders think and feel is never easy and it takes time.

The eating disorders charity beat has lots more information and support services for both people affected by eating disorders as well as their friends and family.

*22 April 2017*

⇨ The above information is reprinted with kind permission from NHS Choices. Please visit www.nhs.uk for further information.

# Clean-eating backlash: how to find nutritional information you can trust

## 'When it comes to food, everyone thinks they are an expert.'

*By Natasha Hinde*

It's 2017 and clean-eating is facing a storm of scrutiny. The hugely successful healthy eating trend has seen a major backlash.

Clean-eating – where people avoid processed foods, sugar and gluten in favour of fruit, vegetables and wholegrains – has been spearheaded by numerous foodies with large social media followings.

The problem is, some of these so-called healthy eating gurus might not have any nutritional qualifications. In fact, with social media, anyone can share dietary advice online.

A new survey by Sainsbury's found that one in five 11- to 14-year-olds now look to bloggers and social media stars for information on healthy eating. Of the 2,000 youngsters surveyed, 43% believe cutting out a food group will lead to a healthy lifestyle.

To combat growing uncertainty surrounding dietary advice, we spoke to experts about the best way to track down nutritional information you can trust.

The clean-eating industry is now worth £590 million. But many have noted that there is a dark side to the trend.

The idea of 'good' and 'bad' foods has been criticised. At worst, clean-eating has been linked to orthorexia – an eating disorder characterised by "an unhealthy obsession with eating healthy food".

Ella Mills, famously known as Deliciously Ella, and the Hemsley + Hemsley sisters have distanced themselves from the term, with Mills reportedly removing all mentions of clean-eating from her website. Alice Liveing, aka Clean-Eating Alice has said she will be keeping her brand name, but she acknowledges that the term is problematic and seeks to promote a balanced approach to eating.

Mills recently starred in a BBC documentary, alongside biochemist Dr Yeo, who explained that the 'clean' part of clean-eating has become too "complicated and loaded".

"When I first read the term, it meant natural, unprocessed," said Dr Yeo. "Now it doesn't mean that at all. It means diet. It means fad."

Dr Yeo isn't the only person to brand the trend as a fad diet. Last year, three students from King's College London launched a campaign called Fight The Fads to "address and correct misinformation in the media to remove the fear and confusion over nutrition". Clean-eating was very much on the agenda.

More recently, they released a petition to legally protect the title 'nutritionist' which has so far garnered more than 6,000 signatures.

In light of this, we spoke to experts about how to get nutritional information from those you can trust.

## 1. Check advice

In the first instance, registered nutritionist Charlotte Stirling-Reed said people need to be wary of what advice is being given to them and question it.

"I would say to check out what claims are being made," she told HuffPost UK. "If they sound too good to be true or are very clear cut when it comes to nutrition, it's very unlikely to be from a registered nutritionist.

"Additionally if they are promoting or pushing a detox, cleanse or 'superfood' you need to be wary."

A registered nutritionist will usually have an undergraduate or post-graduate degree in a nutritional science, plus approximately three years professional experience.

Stirling-Reed explained that nutritionists have to weigh up scientific research along with Government guidelines before they make any recommendations or give advice, meaning they are "more likely to talk about balance and variety than cancer cures or foods with super powers".

## 2. Search a directory

People looking for a trusted professional can find registered nutritionists through the Association For Nutrition.

"However keep in mind that this is a voluntary register, and it is not compulsory for someone calling themselves a 'nutritionist' to be signed up to this register," a British Dietetic Association (BDA) spokesperson told HuffPost UK.

They add that for someone to legally use the title 'dietitian', they must be on the HCPC register.

According to the Association For Nutrition, the title of 'dietician' is the only one that is protected by law, as you must complete one of the HCPC's approved degree programmes to be given the title.

While this is great news for dieticians, it also means that other titles in the nutritional field may be open to abuse.

"There is no statutory protection for any other title in the nutrition field, so no other job titles are legally protected," an Association For Nutrition spokesperson said.

"However the UK Voluntary Register of Nutritionists (UKVRN) was set up to provide a way for the public and employers to be able to distinguish nutrition professionals who can demonstrate that they meet high standards relating to their level of nutrition science knowledge and its application in professional practice."

People who register on the UKVRN have a minimum of degree level nutrition science. Many of them have Masters degrees or PhDs in nutrition too.

## 3. Look out for initials

New graduates with less than three years experience can register as registered associate nutritionists – and then use 'ANutr' after their name.

After an individual gains enough experience to be able to demonstrate the sustained evidence-based application of their knowledge in professional practice and their professionalism, they can then apply to become a registered nutritionist (RNutr).

According to Charlotte Stirling-Reed, the simplest way to tell who is qualified quickly is by checking the initials after their name.

"Hopefully you can spot them as they will be referred to as a registered nutritionist – not a therapist, food expert or guru – and have the letters 'RNutr' after their name," she said.

"When it comes to food, everyone thinks they are an expert. But make sure you're getting advice from someone who really is an expert when it comes to nutrition and your health."

*3 February 2017*

# 'Garment project' removes size labels from clothes giving eating disorder patients chance to recover

*They "empower patients by providing them with new clothing, individualised for their healthy bodies".*

*By Natasha Hinde*

A woman recovering from an eating disorder has turned her negative experiences into something positive, with the help of her close friend.

Erin Drischler is the co-founder of Garment Project, a non-profit organisation which removes size labels from new clothing and then gifts those items to women recovering from eating disorders.

"We are not just giving clothing that fits, we are allowing our client to build confidence in other aspects of her life while tackling the worst part– body image," she explains on the organisation's website.

Drischler knows about the intense cycle of negativity which comes hand-in-hand with clothing sizes all too well.

"After about a decade into my eating disorder, I could start to pinpoint things that were keeping me sick," she recalled. "Every time I would go through treatment, I would lose all sense of self since my core beliefs about food and life were being stripped from me.

"After months of hard work, I would return home to a closet full of clothes that at one point filled me with such

(false) confidence, I would find myself unconsciously striving to fit back into them."

She said the clothes in her wardrobe ranged in sizes, but a lot of them brought back negative memories.

"I could not afford to buy myself a brand new wardrobe - treatment is expensive," she continued.

"Trying on clothes was overwhelming and quickly revealed my new size. In addition to all the other pressures I faced upon arriving home, I didn't have a chance."

Knowing there were many other women in society who would be feeling the same way, she decided to launch Garment Project with her friend Jordan Tomb.

The organisation saves treatment and rehabilitation centres time and resources, by removing all tags and sizing information from clothes prior to shipping them directly to clients.

Drischler and Tomb partner with treatment centres in the US to "empower outgoing patients by providing them with new clothing, individualised for their healthy bodies".

When a woman is nearing the end of inpatient recovery, the treatment

team will communicate accurate measurements along with style and personality information to the Garment team.

With this information, each woman will be guaranteed a basics package, which will includes t-shirts, bras, underwear and jeans.

They will hand-pick items based on the information given to them about the client's personality and lifestyle. They then send the treatment team a link to a personalised, secure web page that the client can shop from.

The organisation, which relies on monetary donations from the general public and contributions from large corporations, primarily helps women in recovery from eating disorders. However, they hope to extend their services to men too.

*15 May 2017*

# Retailers must be more responsible – Be Real responds to Topshop's ultra-thin mannequins

***Two years after Topshop said it would stop its use of ultra-skinny mannequins they reappeared in a shop window. Read our full response.***

Denise Hatton, Chief Executive of the National Council of YMCAs, a founding partner of body image campaign Be Real, said:

"It's shocking to see the return of ultra-thin mannequins at Topshop, almost two years after the retailer said it will stop using them.

"Once again young women and girls are presented with an 'ideal' body type that's unrealistic and unhealthy for the majority of people to achieve.

"Only ever seeing one body type in fashion advertising, particularly an extremely thin body type, risks creating an insidious pressure to attempt to become something we're not.

"This is why we launched the Body Image Pledge last year to urge the advertising, fashion, media and music industries to be responsible in the way they portray body image.

"While many clothing brands and retailers have started to reflect society's diversity in their advertising recently, reintroducing underweight mannequins back to the high street risks undoing all the great progress we've achieved over the last few years."

*6 April 2017*

⇨ The above information is reprinted with kind permission from Be Real. Please visit www.berealcampaign.co.uk for further information.

---

# *To The Bone*: why Netflix's portrayal of eating disorders has got it all wrong

***An article from* The Conversation.**

*By Su Holmes, Reader in TV Studies, University of East Anglia*

THE CONVERSATION

Not many films come with a health warning. But the recent Netflix film *To The Bone*, which tells the story of 20-year-old Ellen – played by Lily Collins – and her journey through treatment for anorexia, has received just that. The UK's national eating disorder charity Beat said in a statement:

"We would strongly urge anyone that might be at risk of an eating disorder to think very carefully before watching this film."

There have also been calls to ban the film because of fears the film might incite eating disorders, or make someone's problem worse.

Eating disorder sufferers – particularly young girls – have long been presented as especially 'vulnerable' to the power of media images and messages. The 'anorexic' is often shown as not simply vain, but also unable to separate image from 'reality'. And research has shown that people diagnosed with anorexia are routinely presented as

being 'suggestively vulnerable' – that is, more likely to be influenced by media images, particularly images of (often unttainable) bodies.

But while these cautions most likely come from a place of genuine concern, they can often have the opposite effect and further trivialise anorexia.

## Models in magazines

Unwittingly or otherwise, debates such as those over *To The Bone* perpetuate the idea that girls can be "infected" with anorexia by looking at images of very slim (or starved) bodies – and that this is where the crux of anorexia lies.

But as my own research with people who have experience of an eating disorder shows, not only do such ideas massively simplify the complex reasons why anorexia may develop, they also trivialise it. As one of the people in my research group explained:

So [it is] less like, well there's a model, a skinny model in a magazine, looking at that, you've been looking at that too

much and so you just wanna be like them... I don't agree with that at all. I think that completely trivialises it.

One of the key problems is that there is inadequate understanding of the social and cultural aspects of eating disorders – both in wider society and the media – as well as in the treatment of eating disorders.

Eating disorders are now understood to combine biological, psychological and social factors, and yet the 'social' part of the equation is still often marginalised in treatment. So although eating disorders have historically been recognised as primarily affecting girls and women in Western societies, contemporary eating disorder treatment does little to look at the relationship between eating problems and cultural constructs of femininity – notwithstanding the 'obvious' fact that most patients are female.

This is despite the wealth of evidence from feminist approaches over the last 40 years which point to the significance of society – and especially gender roles – in the development of eating issues.

These approaches also aim to move beyond the idea of eating disorders as "body image" problems caused by reading too many women's magazines – and instead look at the complex ways eating disorders might play out inequalities between genders on a broader scale.

## Societal expectation

Some of the objections raised about *To The Bone* claim that it glamorises anorexia, and that it privileges the conventional stereotype of a young, white, fragile 'waif'. I for one would like to see more representations that challenge and expand our understanding of what eating disorders "are" in terms of social and cultural identity, and how they might address the stigmatisation and trivialisation of eating disorders, and improve treatment. I don't see this in *To The Bone*.

In fact, as *The Guardian* journalist, Hadley Freeman's excellent article on the film observes, it perpetuates some of the same gender inequities that are behind eating disorders in the first place. Consider, for example, the fact that Keanu Reeves plays "the brilliant, patriarchal medical professional who can fix women".

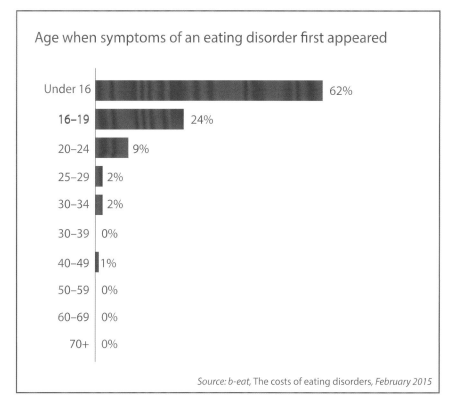

Age when symptoms of an eating disorder first appeared

| Age | % |
|---|---|
| Under 16 | 62% |
| 16–19 | 24% |
| 20–24 | 9% |
| 25–29 | 2% |
| 30–34 | 2% |
| 30–39 | 0% |
| 40–49 | 1% |
| 50–59 | 0% |
| 60–69 | 0% |
| 70+ | 0% |

*Source: b-eat, The costs of eating disorders, February 2015*

The title To The Bone suggests something about getting to the 'truth' of anorexia. Such a possibility is inevitably flawed, as there are many different ways 'anorexia' can be viewed and many different experiences of having anorexia.

As someone who lived with the horrifying and debilitating realities of anorexia for over 20 years, I certainly found little sense of my 'truth' here.

And I'm mad as hell that nobody talked to me about gender during all the time that I was in treatment, or tried to understand what I might have been struggling against. I had to figure this out myself – five years after I was discharged from in-patient treatment. I now know that my anorexia was bound up very clearly with expectations surrounding what it meant to be a "woman", and all that adult femininity may entail. It wasn't rocket science.

I still hope for a film that can show such understandings. But in a climate where feminism is as much vilified as welcomed, and with the skinny female body still being spectacularly fetishised in a film that purports to portray the 'true' horrors of anorexia, I may well have a long wait ahead of me.

*26 July 2017*

⇨ The above information is reprinted with kind permission from *The Conversation*. Please visit www.theconversation.com for further information.

# Key facts

- A 2015 report commissioned by Beat estimates more than 725,000 people in the UK are affected by an eating disorder. Eating disorders tend to be more common in certain age groups, but they can affect people of any age. (page 2)

- Around one in 250 women and one in 2,000 men will experience anorexia nervosa at some point. The condition usually develops around the age of 16 or 17. (page 2)

- Bulimia is around two to three times more common than anorexia nervosa, and 90% of people with the condition are female. It usually develops around the age of 18 or 19. (page 2)

- Anorexia has the highest mortality rate of any psychiatric disorder, from medical complications associated with the illness as well as suicide. Research has found that 20% of anorexia sufferers will die prematurely from their illness. Bulimia is also associated with severe medical complications, and binge eating disorder sufferers often experience the medical complications associated with obesity. (page 5)

- The weight-loss industry in Australia is worth over $635 million. (page 10)

- Most of us get enough protein by eating a well-balanced diet and varying the foods we eat every day, so there is no need to worry too much about getting enough. (page 14)

- Clean Eating Alice, 23, is a big name in the [clean eating] game. Alice isn't vegetarian but her diet is very low in carbohydrate. She claims that her diet and exercise regime has immeasurably improved her health and happiness. It was reported that through her version of clean eating and intensive exercise, she dropped 2st 7lb (16kg) and reduced her body fat percentage from 30% to just 15%. (page 17)

- According to the charity Anorexia and Bulimia Care, anorexia most commonly develops around the age of 16 or 17, while bulimia mainly affects females aged between 16 and 40. (page 18)

- The number of adult men being admitted to hospital with an eating disorder has risen by 70% over the past six years – the same rate of increase as among women. (page 20)

- Data shows that men still account for a small proportion of the total patients diagnosed in hospital, with 1,098 male adults and children admitted in 2015–16 and 12,054 female adults and children. More than 300 boys and girls aged 12 or under were admitted to hospital with an eating disorder in 2015–16. (page 21)

- An estimated 1.6 million people in the UK have experienced an eating disorder. In the US, these figures are as high as 20 million women and 10 million men. (page 22)

- Up to one in five people with chronic anorexia may die as a result of their illness, either due to the direct effects of starvation and malnutrition or due to suicide, making it the deadliest of all psychiatric disorders. Although scientists have made tremendous progress in decoding the underlying biology of eating disorders and in finding ways to intervene in cases of teenage anorexia before the disorder becomes chronic, this hasn't translated into effective treatments for adults. (page 29)

### Anorexia Athletica

An eating disorder and mental health condition that involves excessively exercising in order to lose weight.

### Anorexia Nervosa

An eating disorder and mental health condition that involves an immoderate restriction on food intake.

### Binge Eating Disorder

An eating disorder where a person feels compelled to consume large quantities of food in a short period of time, often when they are not hungry.

### Body Dysmorphic Disorder

A mental health condition where a person has an excessive concern over their body image and what they perceive as their 'flaws'.

### Bulimia Nervosa

An eating disorder and mental health condition that involves excessive food consumption followed by actions such as vomiting or the use of laxatives to compensate for their food intake.

### Clean eating

Generally speaking, 'clean eating' involves eating whole foods like fruit, vegetables and grains, healthy fats, lean meat and unprocessed food. There are concerns that this kind of strict dietary plan can link to developing an eating disorder.

### Diabulimia

An eating disorder in which people with Type 1 diabetes deliberately give themselves less insulin than they need in order to lose weight.

### Disordered eating

A term used to describe eating habits that can be considered `irregular' but do not warrant diagnosis as anorexia or bulimia nervosa.

### Eating disorder

A term used to describe a range of psychological disorders that involve disturbed eating habits such as anorexia or bulimia nervosa.

### Faddy eating

Similar to fussy eating; often involves the exclusion or avoidance of certain foods for no discernible reason.

### Gluten

A protein that is found in foods processed from wheat and other grains.

### Humanitarian Intervention

When a state uses military force against another state whose military action is violating citizens` human rights.

### Orthorexia Nervosa

An eating disorder and mental health condition characterised by an extreme avoidance of food that the sufferer considers to be unhealthy.

### Pica

A disorder that involves the consumption of non-nutritive substances such as dirt, hair or sand.

### Pro-ana

The promotion of eating disorders such as anorexia nervosa as a lifestyle choice.

### Protorexia

An unhealthy fixation with protein-rich foods and supplements, such as diet or muscle-building shakes.

### Thinspiration

Images or videos of women that are slim or of an unhealthy weight as an `inspiration` for weight-loss or for the promotion of eating disorders.

# Assignments

## Brainstorm

⇨ Brainstorm what you know about eating disorders:

- What are some of the different types of eating disorders?

- Who is at risk of suffering from an eating disorder?

## Research

⇨ Research 'Eating Disorders Not Otherwise Specified' and feedback to your class about what you find.

⇨ Research eating disorder charities and organisations who offer young people advice. Make a bullet point list and compare with a classmate's.

⇨ Conduct a questionnaire amongst your year group to find out how many people have heard of or tried 'clean eating'. Ask at least five questions and create a series of graphs or pie charts to show your findings.

⇨ Research the musical figure Karen Carpenter, who tragically died after a long struggle with the eating disorder anorexia. Write a blog post exploring Karen's life and the consequences of her disorder.

## Design

⇨ Choose an article from this book and create an illustration to highlight its key themes.

⇨ Create a leaflet explaining the signs and symptoms of anorexia nervosa.

⇨ Design an app that young people could use to ask questions and seek support if they have a friend who they think might be suffering from an eating disorder.

⇨ Create a questionnaire for young people who are worried that they might have an eating disorder. To take this further, think about how you might turn your questionnaire into an app. What would you call your app? What would the logo be? Would you include helpline numbers at the end? Design your app.

⇨ Draw your ideal mannequin – think carefully about what kind of size and shape they would be, or perhaps you'd even have more than one?

## Oral

⇨ 'Fox & Moon' diet planners may "exacerbate eating disorders". Read the short article on page 18 that discusses this headline then, in small groups, discuss whether you agree. Nominate someone to write a list of your key points and then feedback to the rest of your class.

⇨ Eating disorders are made worse by social media. Debate this statement as a class, with half arguing in favour and half arguing against.

⇨ In pairs, create a PowerPoint presentation that explains the risks of extreme clean eating regimes and suggests healthy alternatives. Perhaps include some research into celebrities who advocate for such diets, and their qualifications (or lack of!)

⇨ Choose an illustration from this book and, in pairs, discuss what the artist was trying to show with their cartoon.

⇨ In pairs, discuss the following questions: What is disordered eating? How does it relate to eating disorders?

⇨ In small groups, create a presentation about the risks of disordered eating that would be suitable for a school assembly. You should explain the problems surrounding disordered eating and make sure that you include a section on healthy eating habits. You could also produce handouts.

## Reading/Writing

⇨ Write a blog post arguing that size labels should be removed from clothes. Use the article on page 37 as a starting point.

⇨ Write an open letter to high-street clothes shops, imploring them to stop using ultra-thin mannequins in their shop windows.

⇨ Read the article on page 38 *To The Bone: why Netflix's portrayal of eating disorders has got it all wrong*. Write an opinion piece for your school newspaper, arguing that it is important for issues such as eating disorders to be tackled on film.

⇨ Imagine that you are an Agony Aunt/Uncle who has received a letter from the parent of a 13-year-old. This parent is worried that their son/daughter has an eating disorder. Write a reply to them, giving advice on how to handle the situation.

⇨ Read the book *Massive* by Julia Bell. Write a review of the book, exploring how well you think the author deals with the topic of eating disorders and whether you think the characters' struggles are realistic.

⇨ Write a definition of the term 'protorexia'.

# Acknowledgements

The publisher is grateful for permission to reproduce the material in this book. While every care has been taken to trace and acknowledge copyright, the publisher tenders its apology for any accidental infringement or where copyright has proved untraceable. The publisher would be pleased to come to a suitable arrangement in any such case with the rightful owner.

## Images

All images courtesy of iStock except page 16 © Monstruo Estrudio, page 24 © Freestocks, page 25 © Alejandro Escamilla-Tenedores, page 26: Unsplash and page 21: Morgue File.

## Icons

Icons on page 4 were made by Freepik from www.flaticon.com.

## Illustrations

Don Hatcher: pages 10 & 22. Simon Kneebone: pages 12 & 32. Angelo Madrid: pages 15 & 39.

## Additional acknowledgements

Editorial on behalf of Independence Educational Publishers by Cara Acred.

With thanks to the Independence team: Shelley Baldry, Tina Brand, Sandra Dennis, Jackie Staines and Jan Sunderland.

Cara Acred

Cambridge, September 2017